MODELLING
SHIPS IN
BOTTLES

MODELLING SHIPS IN BOTTLES

Jack Needham

Patrick Stephens, Wellingborough

First published in 1985

British Library Cataloguing in Publication Data

Needham, Jack
    How to go modelling ships in bottles.———
    2nd expanded ed.
    1. Ship models in bottles
    I. Title   II. Needham, Jack. Modelling ships
    in bottles

    745.592'8   VM298

    ISBN 0-85059-729-3

Photoset in 10 on 11 pt Times, by MJL
Limited, Hitchin, Herts. Printed in Great
Britain on 115 gsm Fineblade coated cartridge,
and bound, by Butler & Tanner Limited,
Frome, Somerset, for the publishers, Patrick
Stephens Limited, Denington Estate,
Wellingborough, Northants, NN8 2QD,
England.

Contents

Foreword

by Alan Villiers

Mr Jack Needham's book on the subject of making small ship models to fit into bottles, and getting them in and tautly rigged, is the most comprehensive, thorough and clear exposition of that skill which I have seen. Indeed, there used to be little written on the subject at all, for it was a sort of seamen's secret and left to them. There have been ship and boat models of some sort or other—by no means all crude or elementary—for 4,000 years, which is far longer than there have been glass bottles. Skins used to serve well enough to contain liquids, then pottery and metal. No early Semitic, Chinese, Japanese or Nordic mariner seems to have thought of putting a crude ship model in a skin wine-carrier: probably he had better use for both. As far as one may discover, the skill of bottling small ship models is comparatively new even among seamen and, among landsmen, very new indeed.

There could be a lot of leisure in well-run old-time sailing ships for the reason that they had to go to sea with large crews to man their guns, handle their sails, and replace their casualties if only to scurvy. Seamen were handy men by the nature of their calling, making their own clothes and much concerned with the fine skills of ropework and sailmaking. A good ship was most popular among them, and they tried their hands at primitive models of her (the beautiful old models we see in museums were made by designers and great shipwrights ashore as a vital part of the building process). What horny-handed ingenious old mariner pioneered the skill of getting a hinge-masted little model into a wide-necked bottle and setting up her elementary rigging inside the glass, no one will ever know; or when. By the time I got to sea the skill was long established though—as far as I know—not at all then practised ashore except maybe in old seamen's homes. It was a trade winds dogwatch pastime in happy ships. Some older hand would go to work, with a convenient bottle, a bit of well-seasoned wood and some thread. In time he would need some putty from 'Chips' to make his sea, and a few old pins for hinges to step the masts, a bit of crude paint from the boatswain's locker—that was all, and a lot of patience and skill. Once started, soon the whole watch would be at work. I had a 'bash' once myself aboard the *Herzogin Cecilie*.

It was easy enough to grasp the principles of the thing, producing first a reasonable small model outside the bottle with the masts and yards trimly folded back in the fore-and-aft line, to be hauled carefully into place inside the bottle by means of the fore-and-aft stays left loose for the purpose. But I was a left-handed model maker. I am well content to leave such skills to an expert like Mr Needham, whose thorough treatise, with its lucid explanations, excellent diagrams and photographs, makes me inclined, indeed, to sit down and have another 'go' myself. It is a first-rate job.

The author

Jack Needham has been making ships in bottles for more than 50 years. Born in 1916 in Sheffield, he attended two distinctly ancient council schools and completed his education in an Intermediate school at the age of 14. His best subjects at school were English and French, and on one occasion he even received 98 per cent for the latter subject, probably due to the strong 'crush' he had for the rather curvaceous teacher. He left school in 1930, which was not an ideal time in view of the employment situation which then prevailed, it being difficult to find a job of any kind. His first situation was as an errand boy for a grocer's shop, a job which paid 6/- a week and entailed working from 7.30 am until the last orders had been delivered, and the depredations of a large colony of mice had been obliterated from the tops of the open flour and sugar sacks, (a far cry from to-day's hygienically-wrapped foodstuffs). Even in those difficult days this type of labour seemed to Jack Needham to be akin to slavery, so, after a fortnight, he found employment in the electrical trade. This job, besides offering an increase in salary (bringing his weekly pay up to the princely sum of 7/6), included such intellectually straining tasks as sweeping up, brewing tea and 'topping up' and charging 'wireless' batteries. After some months of working for an extremely frugal employer, whose more charming attributes included leaving halfpennies strewn on the floor to test his employees' honesty (which, one night, were all screwed to the floor by an employee who was under 'notice'), he switched to the printing trade where he worked until taking early retirement at the age of 64.

Jack Needham has always been keen on the outdoor life so, once he had left school, he started camping and cycling. He competed in his first cycling time-trial at the age of 17, with his last fling at competition riding being in 1961, when he was 44. In 1940 Jack was called up for service in the Royal Navy, eventually reaching the dizzy heights of seaman torpedoman, after years of working with maximum effort in conditions of minimum comfort. Covering over 70,000 sea-miles he visited Iceland, Canada, Bermuda, Trinidad, Jamaica, Africa, India, Java and the Cocos Island, to name but a few, and since then has toured France, Belgium, Luxembourg, Holland and Germany.

Demobbed in 1946, Jack returned to the printing trade and resumed his cycle-racing. In 1948 he competed against the then World Champion, Reg Harris, a race which affected Harris' position not one jot. At about this time Jack also resumed the less energetic, but rather more rewarding pastime of putting ships in bottles, a hobby he had originally taken up at the age of 14. His models have been exhibited in four London Exhibitions, hundreds of Craft Fairs and there are many examples of his work in museums in the UK, America, Africa, France and Israel. After years of demonstrating this craft at local shows he was invited by the *Daily Express* to display his craft at the International Boat Show at Earls Court in January 1969, and in 1971 he exhibited at the *Sheffield—City on the move* show at the Royal Exchange, London. His initial venture as an author was the article *In a glass of its own*, which appeared in *Do It Yourself* magazine in February 1972, followed by his first book *Modelling Ships in Bottles* published by Patrick Stephens Ltd in September of that year. The first publication of this book appeared in UK and American editions and proved so popular that it was subsequently translated into Spanish, Italian, Swedish, Dutch and German. Jack still lives in Sheffield but even though he misses the sea feels he has too many roots to leave the district. (One of his ancestors, William Needham de Stanton, lived about 20 miles away from Sheffield in the year 1103.)

Since retiring Jack has spent his time in replying to some 500 letters annually, model making, lecturing and exhibiting his work at various local shows and doing the odd spot of maintenance on the family car. Always a great believer in holidays he and his wife get away to the coast when the opportunity arises and Jack still cycles about 100 miles every week. He enjoys the odd weekend pint with friends at the local pub but people who ask him, 'How do you crack the bottoms off bottles to get the ships in?' are inclined to receive an answer in basic Anglo-Saxon. The Needhams have a grown-up daughter, two grandchildren and an extremely comical tortoise of unknown age, who has lived with them for over 25 years and rejoices in the name of 'Osbert Nerk'. This odd creature, who scuttles into a corner at the first onset of cold weather, receives cards at Christmas and once scared the pants off a television team who had come to the house to do a programme on Sheffield craftsmen. Jack likes good music, whether it be Chopin, Debussey, Grieg, Glenn Miller or talented groups such as Abba. He watches TV selectively, considers Buster Keaton the greatest comedian of all time, (with the exception of certain politicians who, perforce, remain anonymous) and likes *Tom & Jerry*, which he often watches with his grandchildren. Jack is persuaded that everyone should have a hobby of some kind, whether it be sport, gardening, marquetry, painting or philately and thus feels sorry for people who say that they are bored, as there are so many rewarding hobbies which can give a real sense of achievement. To this end he trusts this book will prove to be of help.

Preface

Since the publication of the original edition of *Modelling Ships in Bottles* in 1972, many readers will have embarked on the enthralling hobby of making ship models to put in bottles and will, no doubt, have had their appetites whetted for even more unusual and intricate forms of bottle modelling. Therefore part of this extended second edition is intended for those people who have already become proficient in the ships-in-bottles field and appreciate that practically any model can be put into a bottle, no matter how 'impossible' the undertaking may appear at first. Models such as cars, aircraft, railway engines, windmills etc can be inserted in bottles, as can wooden puzzles, ladders and chairs. The possibilities are practically unlimited. The main thing to remember is that all objects have to be built up in segments each one of which must be smaller than the bottle-neck aperture and which have to be united inside the bottle by means of dowels and glue to form the complete model.

All components for 'figure' models must be made as accurately as possible and, should the model maker be in any doubt, it is better to make the model on the small side, thus making ample allowance for the paint or varnish finishes. Some people would, perhaps, only use glue but the use of dowel pegs ensures that the pieces are in their exact position. The reader will appreciate of course, that figure models, unlike ship models, have no threads or excess rigging to act as 'remote controls' but that the components are placed in the bottle one at a time, each piece being joined to its fellow individually. So it follows that these models do take a little longer than ships to put in bottles as only a limited amount of construction can be done at any one time, due to the fixing and drying out which is vital at each stage. Should construction be rushed the modeller may well have problems with condensation after the model is completed; a problem which is practically impossible to eradicate once it occurs. However, any person of average model-making ability can construct satisfactory figure models providing the rules of assembly are observed and a modicum of patience exercised.

The advantages of enclosing a model in a bottle are manifold and since a rigid model inside a narrow-necked bottle looks absolutely 'impossible' it will immediately arouse interest and provide a subject for discussion. On the practical side they are completely dust and damp proof and will, with reasonable treatment, last forever. A glass-case, unless perfectly built, can look a trifle out of place in a home and glass-cases by virtue of their weight are particularly susceptible to damage. At this point it might be as well to mention that *all* bottle models,

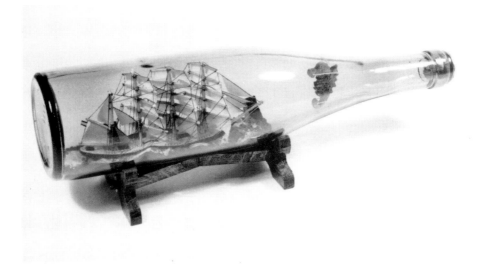

Four-masted barque by the author, in brown-tinted hock bottle, with a 'sea horse' in the bottle neck.

whether of ships or figures must never be put in an unduly warm place, such as a fireside shelf, or on a window ledge which is subject to strong light as this will (with the bottle acting like a burning glass) inevitably result in unsightly discolouration or fading. With careful handling there is no reason why your models should not last forever. Though ships and other models in bottles may look fragile, they will stand any amount of handling if properly treated and many of mine have made journeys of thousands of miles, some even going by parcel post to the North American Exposition in San Diego, California in 1982 and arrived back completely intact. Others have survived many hurried journeys to London in the boot of the car and I have yet to carry out any repairs! My sole casualty has been a model sent to an enthusiast in the south of England and this must have fallen from one of the vans, for it was returned in about 300 pieces. Still, after 52 years of model making, that is not a bad casualty rate.

Acknowledgements

It is natural when compiling a book of this type that the author comes into contact with people of like interests. All the people I have met or to whom I have written have been most helpful, especially museum or library officials both at home or abroad and to these kind people, who are far too numerous to mention individually, I wish to express my sincere thanks. To single out the people who have been of outstanding help is extremely difficult, but one person who has been of immense help is Leonard Tipper, Special Events Organiser of the *Daily Express*. It was entirely due to him that I was invited to participate in the 1969 International Boat Show at Earls Court, London, which was a great help in my becoming known in this rather specialised field of modelling. So many people at the Show asked where they could obtain a book on the subject that it was their enquiries that led me to write *Modelling Ships in Bottles*, published by Patrick Stephens Limited in 1972. To Patrick Stephens and his many helpful colleagues I also owe a debt of gratitude for their help and forebearance, suggestions as to layout and format and assistance with some of the photography. Since the publication of the first edition many hundreds of people from all over the world have written to express their appreciation. Many of the letters are from retired people who need a new interest in life, others from schoolboys or ladies (whose dainty dexterity with other hobbies such as sewing, knitting etc has found a new application). Putting ships and models in bottles is a hobby that requires patience and a lightness of touch, although many folk, including myself, have fingers like a bunch of bananas but this need not be a handicap to a keen builder!

In the 12 years since the first edition was published, many Associations such as the European Association of Ships in Bottles, the International Ships in Bottles Association (America) and the Japanese Ships in Bottles Association have gradually grown in number and in members. There are also 'lone' modellers, many of whom are Lifeboatmen, Lighthouse Keepers or individuals who live in isolated places, such as the Orkney and Shetland Islands. Many a winter's night must be spent in making ship models and almost daily I receive letters from new enthusiasts who, through the help of a book like this, have taken up the old seafarer's hobby, which up to now was in danger of becoming a lost art. I must also thank those many people who have described my book as 'The classic work on the subject' and who have produced some really outstanding models which, besides showing excellent workmanship, display great originality and ingenuity.

Author's models of a big brig and a 'baby' brig in brandy bottles.

To all pen friends of long standing I would like to express my gratitude. These include Major Chris Nair of Jabalpur, my oldest and very first ship-in-bottle correspondent; Aubrey Dunning, an ex-Merchant Navy man and excellent ship modeller who lives in Utrecht; Bill Dawe, late of the 'Glorious Glosters' who lives in the West Country, a man of great modesty and outstanding ability in this field and whom I rate amongst the best in the world; John Burden, a good friend who lives in Wiltshire and who turns out some excellent models; Max Truchi of Marseilles and Don Hubbard of Coronado, USA, both fellow authors and keen ship-in-bottle makers; Leon Labistour of Robin Hood's Bay, and his talented wife. Then there is the irrepressible Vic Burley (late RN, like myself) of Brisbane, Australia, an ex-Pompey rating, who makes all types of models in bottles, writes poetry, draws the funniest cartoons and has even built his own house; Edwin Clark of New Zealand, who in between putting ships in bottles has restored a 1929 Essex 'straight eight' into rally-winning condition, has gained acclaim in his own country, also writes regularly and sends photos of his latest models.

Above all there is my wife, Audrey, whose patience, when faced with a table full of model-making impedimenta or nautical books which come tumbling out of the odd cupboard, never ceases to amaze me. It is to her I would like to dedicate this book.

Jack Needham
Sheffield, 1984

Introduction

Some while ago a short article bearing the title *Slowly sinking. . .the art of bottling a ship*, appeared in a popular newspaper. The writer of the article described how an advertising agency had sent out an SOS in London for anyone who could put a ship in a bottle as they wanted a 'shot' of the actual stage when the masts were being pulled up. Apparently they were still searching after the article was published. One or two shops had ready-made models which had been imported from Scandinavian countries and someone else knew of two small firms in the West Country who made miniatures for the Christmas trade, retailing at about 35p each.

A correspondent who was interviewed by the reporter concerned said (and I quote), 'You do this by making everything collapsible' (I hope he didn't include the hull!). 'You then pull up the masts and try to make the cotton invisible.' By this I assume he meant the excess rigging threads, not the actual rigging which is, to say the least, essential. He then went on to say, 'In fact, nearly all the most intricate ones were made by cheating. In the good old ships-in-bottles days they cut out the bottom and got a glass blower to fuse it back on'.

Personally speaking, as a ship model maker of 50 years' practical experience, I have never read such a ridiculous statement. Having put two-, three-, four-, five-, six- and seven-masted ships in bottles I can see no point in resorting to any methods such as those described. As the melting point of glass is approximately 696°C the reader can judge what would happen to a model made of wood, paper and cotton in *that* temperature! Of course, as with anything intricate, one always comes up against the 'wise guy' who has never even attempted anything as complicated as putting a ship in a bottle, but can tell everybody else how 'they' make them. The favourite explanation usually given by bewildered adults to enquiring children is 'they (the mysterious "they" again) just pull a string'; no mention of hours of carving out a hull to scale, smoothing down, painting and varnishing, rigging, making the masts fold and the yards and sails swivel, to say nothing of fittings such as deck houses, hatches, capstans, boats and—a great asset to any sailing ship—a helm! Nor yet, of course, a mention of the painstaking research necessary for accurate modelling. Other folk say 'They (!) crack the bottom off the bottle and stick it back on.'

The only string I ever use is for making an ornamental 'Turk's Head' knot to finish off a model bottle neck. And as for 'cracking off' bottle bottoms this could be a gory experience and could probably make a very nasty tear in your hand, ruin the carpet, boost sales of Elastoplast and put the family cat out of commission for weeks. Of course, almost everyone has seen those hideous plastic imitations which apparently emanate from Hong Kong and one or two plastic dimple-shape bottles made in two very obvious halves with a plastic 'kit' type ship inside, the whole ensemble being surmounted by a reading lamp. The sight of these would give any mariner worth his salt a severe bout of the shudders.

Having seen so many old sailor-made models in museums and reputable antique shops I can truthfully say that all were absolutely genuine. Some were really remarkable and would stand up to the most minute examination. All credit is due to those nameless mariners who lovingly constructed them in the conditions which prevailed at that time. No person of intelligence would pay the price these old masterpieces are now commanding, or be taken in by fakes. In any case why try to fake one, when one can get the 'know how' from this book? Like the ivory chessmen one sees with a perfectly round ball inside, all made from *one* piece of material, there's a way of making intricate articles. For ships in bottles all you will require is a modicum of patience, the right tools and an ability to face some disappointments, possibly, while you master the techniques. Eventually, however, a finished model, well made, will be your reward and your leisure time will have been well spent. Bear in mind that nothing good can be made in a hurry. Personally I have always found ships in bottles to be a fascinating hobby and get just as big a kick out of completing a ship now as I did with my earlier and much cruder efforts. I hope you, too, will find the same satisfaction.

'Carafology'

There is not, as far as I am aware, a word in any language to describe the art of inserting models into bottles, so I have taken the liberty of concocting one which lends itself to this fascinating pastime. Literally dissected this word is not a precise description of my all-absorbing hobby, but it is a short, self-explanatory word which could, in time, become part of the English language.

Whenever I display my models at any exhibition or craft fair a great deal of interest is generated and for every person who asks the question 'How do ships get in bottles?' there is always another who wonders how and when it all started. Although no one can answer the latter question with any accuracy, it is unlikely that any sailor attempted this before the era of the clipper ships as the hull shapes of vessels prior to this period did not lend themselves to being inserted in a bottle. However, with the coming of the sleek-lined narrow-hulled clipper ships of the mid 1800s, such as were built in America and a few years later in England, some mariner with probably above average intelligence suddenly had the inspiration to put one of these models in a bottle. (Models of ships have been made for thousands of years, some being found in Tutankhamun's tomb, amongst those of other kings of Egypt.) And of course, with their masts, yards and rigging being necessarily fragile, a bottle was an ideal ready-made 'case' in which to protect the model. There would probably be no lack of 'empties' in the fo'c'sle, especially after a Bacchanalian shore leave! A sailor could then carry a model or models in his canvas kit bag with complete safety, to be given to his wife or sweetheart on his return home or, alternatively, the product of many weeks painstaking labour would be sold in some dockside tavern for a mere pittance.

The chance of monetary gain was perhaps a deciding factor in the start of this fascinating hobby as seamen in this particular period were notoriously underpaid, as well as being grossly overworked, and many a model which was built in the dimly-lit, rolling, pitching and crowded fo'c'sle of these ships would later change hands in some dockside pub for a mere fraction of their true value. Other models might find themselves on some old mariner's mantelshelf.

Some of these models were remarkable when one bears in mind the crude materials these first modellers had at their disposal. No fine drills or enamels would be at hand and, of course, ship's paint would be used which would not enhance the overall scale appearance of the miniature.

Other models, understandably, were quite crude and disproportionate as many sailors never had the opportunity of seeing the ship they served on under

Five assorted miniatures, all made by the author, shown with a 1p piece for size comparison. The rectangular bottle in the centre contains a two-masted schooner, two cottages, a windmill, a jetty, a beach and a lighthouse. It measures 2¾ × 1¼ × 1 inch, and the bottle neck diameter is just ¼-inch.

sail from ashore and the length of the hull and height of the masts were unknown to a precise degree, so a lot of guesswork would enter into a model's construction. While working aloft, bending and furling sails, many mariners would naturally get an exaggerated view of the height of the masts, and especially perhaps the helmsmen at the wheel, compelled to keep their eyes on the towering mass of canvas lest their vessel be taken aback or some change of wind direction set the sails all a-shaking. So it is understandable that many of these earlier models left something to be desired. Nevertheless, they were quite remarkable when one imagines under what difficult conditions they were constructed.

The craft of models in bottles, other than ships, would appear to go back much further than people realise. As I stated before, ships in bottles probably began as a craft in itself around the middle of the 19th century but models in bottles would appear to have been on the scene much earlier than that. As a calculated guess I would say that this was originally a landsman's craft, carried out in various parts of the world, possibly by people in religious orders. One such model, of which I have an excellent photograph, depicts a crucifixion scene with the horizontal edges of the cross touching the sides of the bottle, two angels on vertical wires on each side as well as a sponge and lance on thin poles. A large curved nail goes right through the cork on the inside, fitting closely to the curved shoulder of the bottle. This model points to a very highly skilled craftsman. The shape of the bottle and the tiny flaws in the glass indicate that it is very old and it could be about 200 years since this model was made. The art of putting nails through corks—there are three ways of doing this—is described in Chapter 11 of this book. Another variety of model which seems to be well known in both France and Spain contains up to ten horizontal wooden cross pieces on a single vertical 'stalk'. From the horizontal crosses hang many silk wound reels of various colours, all strung together to form a geometrical pattern. The idea of building a model like this is really quite mind-boggling, even to a person already skilled in the bottling art. So, judging by the appearance of the bottles' shape and quality it would appear that these models were the fore-runners of ships in bottles. Whether these were made by people in abbeys or monasteries and *then* seen by sailors who decided they could do the same with a ship we will never know. It is quite possible that ships in bottles began as a separate hobby but since its origins are not really known it is a debatable question and thus open to conjecture.

Many models of a more recent era belong to the 'puzzle' category rather than to the scenic models with quite a few being made in prisons as a pastime. Several years ago I saw quite a few models of chairs, ladders, tables etc which had definitely been made in Parkhurst Prison on the Isle of Wight. The

The author with his unusual model of a sailor putting a model ship in a bottle—in a bottle!—one of his exhibits at the International Boat Show in 1969.

workmanship in these was first class and some were very ingenious. Other modern models have quite amusing themes. An Italian pen-friend of mine, one Cesare Petrillo, has made a very clever bottle model depicting an old-fashioned photographer, complete with black hood and plate camera, taking a 'well posed' picture of a family group, who look as if they are quite dreading the ordeal. Another model of Cesare's is a two-tier scene of the interior of a house, with a small child in bed upstairs (complete to slippers under the bed) whilst on the ground floor the child's parents are sitting on four-legged stools at a gingham covered table eating a meal. The table is laid with crockery, a bottle of wine, glasses, plates, bread and salami while an electric light bulb, with shade, hangs from the ceiling. This inventive builder has also put aircraft, trains and paddle steamers in bottles, with his largest ship model in a 12 gallon bottle! As with models of ships with coastal and harbour backgrounds, the variety of models to be made is endless, so originality should be the aim. Quite often I get inspiration from cartoons and add any embellishments as they spring to mind. Some models I have seen by Japanese enthusiasts are particularly clever; one is of a Roman galley with banks of oars moving in time to piped music; another of a sailing ship which rolls and pitches in the 'sea' by means of slowly rotating magnets while another 'gem' is a four-masted sailing ship in the bottom of a Chianti bottle which has a neck length of about 30 in.

From small beginnings the modeller can go on to tackle the more complicated models, going from strength to strength as his enthusiasm and ability increases. In time his prowess will become a source of astonishment to his friends and every model will be a fresh challenge. If you are ever in London, make a point of visiting the *Cutty Sark* in dry dock at Greenwich. Built in 1869, the same year that the Suez Canal was opened, she is the only complete tea clipper remaining anywhere in the world and, thanks to the foresight of The *Cutty Sark* Society, has been fully restored and is preserved for all time. A visit will teach the would-be ship modeller more than he can learn from half-a-dozen books on the subject and there are some beautiful models on display as well as plans and illustrated handbooks.

The Science Museum in South Kensington also houses a remarkable collection of models, photographs of which can be obtained from the museum at modest prices. Such exhibits are fine inspiration for the would-be ship modeller. The choice of subject is yours, as most of the later types of tea and wool carriers as well as the three-, four- and five-masted barques which carried nitrates from various ports in South America all make neat and attractive models.

Chapter 1

Before you begin

There is an obvious temptation in all modelling hobbies to get something going straight away. This is to be encouraged as there is no substitute for enthusiasm. However, many potential followers for any particular hobby are lost in the early stages for they rush into a project so keenly that they have neglected to equip themselves properly for the task. A well-made model looks deceptively easy and the average tyro has no difficulty in imagining himself adding the last touches to an admirable and excellent model. There is a strong inclination to get hold of the raw materials at once and start carving away. I'm all for this approach so long as the newcomer is well prepared with tools, materials, an idea of what is required, and some inkling of the limitations, both personal and practical, within the hobby.

I hope the reader will resist the temptation to get started at least until after he's read this book through. The great thing, however, is to *make* a start, and with this in mind I've provided practical details for a very simple but pleasing model (see Chapter 3) which I strongly advise all beginners to try first before getting on to more ambitious projects. Remember that ships in bottles are very much a 'craft' hobby. In other words, you start with raw materials and information you find for yourself and not with the luxury of a kit of parts as you might have, say, with a model aircraft.

To start with you need tools, materials and a few handy gadgets, and these I will deal with first. Then you will need an idea of how to go about researching the subject, in other words gathering the drawings, photographs, books, data and other reference material you will need before embarking on the construction of an accurate model.

Tools and materials required
You will need the following tools and materials for successful ship-in-bottle modelling. Most items are readily available quite cheaply and you may indeed already possess quite a few of them.

1. A jeweller's/watchmaker's archimedes drill or a pin chuck and some number 70 and 80 drills.
2. A pair of slim pointed tweezers about 5 in long.
3. A pair of narrow pointed scissors; those used by hairdressers are ideal.
4. A small coil of florist's wire (or similar soft wire), for the mast hinges.
5. About six of the smallest size water colour brushes.

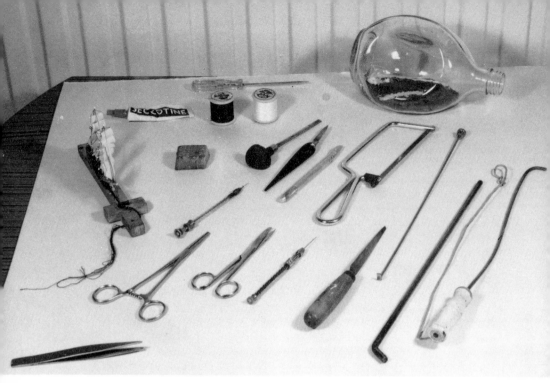

A selection of some of the principal tools needed for modelling ships in bottles.

An ideal folding plastic workbox for modelling requisites, obtainable from Woolworth's or similar outlets.

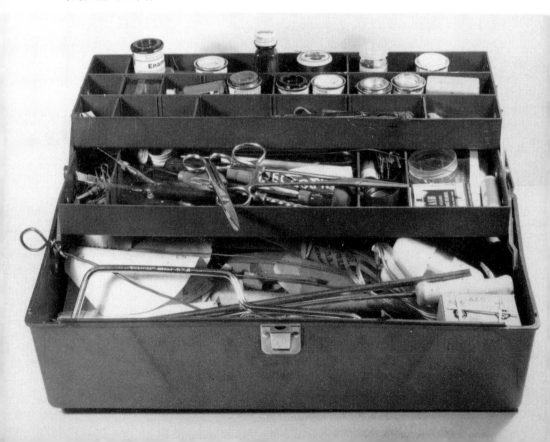

6. A selection of small tins of enamel—white, brown, black, green, red and clear varnish. Humbrol brand paints are excellent and widely available from model shops. There are now some colours specially for ship modellers, including 'scrubbed wood'.

7. Three long wires—bicycle spokes are ideal.

8. A piece of stout iron or steel rod about 12 in × 3/16 in, bent at the end, for putting in your 'sea' and to press your model into whilst erecting the masts.

9. A packet of the finest needles.

10. Reels of black, brown, buff and white Sylko cotton (dressmaking thread).

11. A tube of Copydex or latex-based adhesive. 'Slow' adhesives are preferable as they allow time to make any adjustments.

12. A piece of beeswax—this takes the 'furriness' from the cotton and can be had from ships' chandlers.

13. A sharp scalpel pattern craft knife.

14. A small woodcarver's chisel 3/16 in or 1/4 in wide.

15. Various grades of glasspaper up to 'O' grade.

16. A small steel frame saw and blades, and/or an X-acto razor saw.

17. Some blue and white Plasticine; this is made in 1 lb packets and sold in art shops, but small packets can be had from toyshops.

18. A small pair of pointed pliers, incorporating cutters.

19. A small screw-on vice which can be fastened on to an old table.

20. Some 1/16 in beech dowelling or cocktail sticks for masts and bowsprit.

21. A packet of Chinese toothpicks, ideal for making yards and gaffs.

22. A half-round and a thin flat, fine file.

23. Bottle of 'thinners' for cleaning out paint brushes.

This may seem a pretty formidable list, but the majority of these tools will last a lifetime. In fact, the outlay, even if you were buying the whole lot new, would be much less than the cost of tools for any other constructive hobby. A tin or wooden box makes a handy receptacle in which to keep these tools and materials. Preferably have two, one specifically for the paints, brushes and thinners.

Gadgets

In addition to the tools and materials itemised, there are various useful gadgets which you can fabricate for yourself. I've described these below.

Rigging cutter A fragment of razor blade glued into the split end of a 6 in length of dowel is used to cut off surplus jib stays under the bowsprit. Better still, if you can solder, fasten a blade fragment into a saw cut in a piece of 1/8 in wire. This has the advantage of being easily 'bendable' for awkward cuts. (See fig 1.)

Hinged brush A hinged paint brush for painting the insides of bottles which have a background scene. Simply cut an ordinary water colour brush about an inch above the metal ferrule to a flat section as shown. Cut a corresponding slot in the rest of the paintbrush handle. Drill and fasten with a pin. Also drill through the piece of wood attached to the ferrule in two positions and again in the end of the handle and tie a loop of thin twine as illustrated. You then have a brush which can be moved at any angle to paint the inside of a bottle. (See fig 2.)

Wave-maker A small mustard spoon end fitted into a 3/16 in dowel about 10 in long. This is invaluable for forming 'waves' and smoothing out the white 'wake' astern of your model. (See fig 3.)

Fig 1: *A fragment of razor blade glued to a length of dowel makes a handy rigging cutter.*

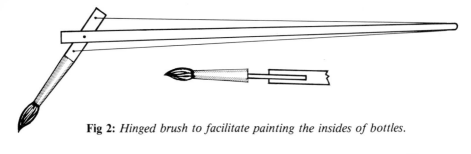

Fig 2: *Hinged brush to facilitate painting the insides of bottles.*

Fig 3: *Spoon attached to rod to form waves in Plasticine 'sea'.*

Left, Fig 4: *Simple gadget for making line grooves in a hull.*

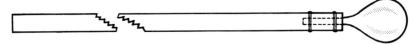

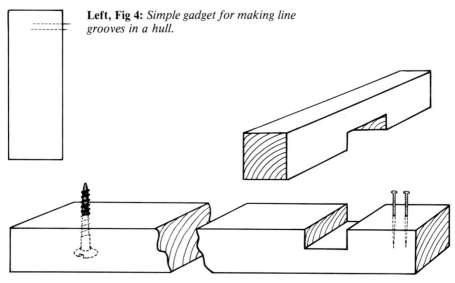

Fig 5: *The rigging base—an essential piece of equipment.*

Fig 6: *An extremely handy gadget made of brass tubing, inside which is a steel rod threaded at one end. By turning A the brass jaws B and C close and grip any small fitting, such as a deck house or hatch, and by unscrewing A one can release fittings where required when the model is inside the bottle. This simple but effective device was given to the author at a London exhibition by a fellow enthusiast.*

Waterline marker For putting a groove for waterline and sheerline on a model using white thread for perfect white lines, a useful little gadget can be made by driving two stout pins in a square piece of wood about ¹/₁₆ in apart. (See fig 4.) The top pin should protrude ⅛ inch and the bottom ¹/₃₂ in. The top pin rests on the sheer of the hull whilst the wood is moved along the hull. This will form a groove parallel to the sheerline. This groove can be smoothed if desired by following it with a very sharp 6H pencil. To make a waterline the 6H pencil method is the best. Screw your model to the rigging base (see below), making sure it is perfectly level and make an indentation ¹/₁₆ in up from the base of your model with the pencil fastened equally firmly. It will be necessary to move the pencil right around the model to mark the stern and bow portions clearly.

Rigging base This is easily made of ¹/₂ in section wood, the longer piece measuring 8 in and the short one 2 in. A simple cross lap joint is made to form a cross and two nails driven in to form a cleat around which you can wind the various items of rigging whilst working on the yards, braces and sails, as the standing rigging must be kept taut at this stage. If necessary put an elastic band over the rigging beyond the cleat. This will prevent any unravelling and consequent slackening of rigging. The screw should be a fairly slack fit. (See fig 5.)

Gripping device A fellow enthusiast kindly presented me with this handy gadget, which you could easily and inexpensively make or have made (see fig 6). It has proved a most useful aid to gripping, inserting and then releasing small fittings when the model is inside the bottle.

Work top Finally let me conclude this section by stating the obvious—that is the need for a good working surface. An old drawing board, possibly covered in part with Formica, would be ideal; part should be left uncovered so that the wood will take pins, etc. An old tray could be used instead. You may, of course, already have a suitable work-bench, but for anyone restricted to the kitchen table, a work top of some sort is essential for cutting and filing.

Research

The importance of research in ship modelling cannot be over-emphasised. A great source of information is, of course, your own public library. Personally, I have always found head librarians most helpful and the lending system, which works countrywide at a reasonable cost for postage to the borrower, is a great asset to the would-be modeller. Most of the famous ships have had several books written about them by various authors and many retired captains in sail have published really comprehensive books about their favourite commands, even including plans. Maritime museums are another good guide and if you are lucky you might find a builder's model of the ship you intend to make. The Science Museum in South Kensington, London, has a really wonderful collection and also a photographic service from which you can buy large photographs of models at very little cost.

Should you ever want to make a model of a West Country schooner a visit to their former ports like Fowey, Par, Polperro, Mevagissey and a whole lot more can bring in plenty of information. Local libraries and museums in these seaports usually yield books and pictures of great reference value. At the turn of the century and often 20 or so years earlier, sometimes all the male members of families sailed as crew and any of their relatives might, for the price of a pint or two in the local, unleash a vertible treasure-house of information about their forebears and the ships they served in. I have experienced this several times, notably after reading Adrian Seligman's very good book, *The Voyage of the Cap Pilar*. This is an absorbing story of how 20 young men sailed round the world on a voyage lasting 25 months, covering almost 40,000 miles, and how subsequently the ship was laid up at Brightlingsea. When war broke out she was towed up to Wivenhoe in Essex and later put into the dry dock at the local shipbuilding yard. About seventeen years ago, I remember going aboard her (I suspect at some personal peril!) with a great deal of sadness to see a mere hulk slowly rotting away but still retaining the beautiful lines she had when she sailed triumphantly into New York almost at the end of her long journey.

She was so well built that her ultimate destruction presented something of a problem. At one time it was considered towing her out to sea at high tide and blowing her up, but eventually most of her timbers were sold, for use as fuel for the ovens of a bakery at Wivenhoe, and the keel is buried in the dry dock there. Yet one of the crew who is a solicitor in Colchester paid a last visit to the ship and obtained two of the bollards which, it was proposed, be placed on the quay at Wivenhoe as a reminder of the last resting place of a barquentine which gave a score of young men an experience they will cherish for the rest of their days.

So, as you can see, this little account shows how fascinating research can be and it is really the most enjoyable way of finding out about the ship of which you propose to build a replica. The Irish Republic was one of the last strongholds of coastal sailing shipping, particularly the east coast, and such ports as Wicklow, Arklow and Wexford could boast quite a number of local sail boats up to and after the Second World War, and many a coastal cottage owner has an original sailor-made ship in bottle or those half hull models mounted on a varnished backboard. The latter are becoming quite rare and valuable.

Exeter is another useful place to visit for it has a really good Maritime Museum and, although this may come as a surprise, so has Whitby (Pannett Park). Other towns with nautical connections up and down the country have museums to provide similar information and inspiration. Museum curators will usually give any information willingly and perhaps in some cases have plans and illustrations of models for sale. Greenwich, as well as being the 'home' of *Cutty Sark*, is also notable for its famous and historic Maritime Museum. In Europe, Amsterdam and Hamburg both have excellent museums, too.

Good rigging and deck plans though are essential if you are to build accurately and, for expenses entailed, well worth the extra cost. It is a comparatively simple operation to scale plans down to the required dimensions and modify rigging to suit the purpose.

The amount of individual reference you need to do will, of course, depend to some extent on your choice of subject. Personal research in museums will certainly enable you to turn up drawings and details of lesser-known ships so that you may well end up with models nobody else has ever made, at least in ship-in-bottle size. If time or distance defeat you—you may live miles from the sea or seaports and your work may not allow you time for visits to museums—the easy alternative, at least in your early endeavours in the hobby, is to model well-known ships (such as *Cutty Sark, Victory* or *Thermopylae*) which are well-documented in books. You should be able to find volumes dealing with at least one of these ships in any large local public library, where you may find several books already on the shelves but any others you know of can certainly be ordered.

There are several specialist books available on certain famous ships. Both

Patrick Stephens and MAP offer good books dealing with HMS *Victory* in considerable detail and between them they cover several other well-known types. MAP Plans Service (13-15 Bridge Street, Hemel Hempstead, Herts) also have ready-made scale drawings of several famous vessels.

By careful choice of subject it would be possible to keep going for several years modelling these famous ships where, subject-for-subject, the amount of research needed is relatively little. While on the subject of books, incidentally, it is worth while mentioning the works of Harold A. Underhill which cover in detail many aspects of masts and rigging (see Appendix 3). For ship-in-bottle modelling these books contain more information than you would actually need but, nonetheless, all books are valuable for reference if they help you to grasp and absorb the subject in depth.

Keep a notebook and scrapbook in which you can paste magazine or newspaper cuttings which relate to ships which interest you. Some libraries offer photostat services for researchers and any such material you get this way can be kept in the scrapbook. Notes on rigging, colours and other relevant details can all be entered so that your scrapbook can become the workbook for the project in hand. Museums allow you to make notes on any of their exhibits and all this kind of material can go in the book. If you have a camera you can take pictures of details which interest you on public exhibits like *Cutty Sark* or *Victory*. Similarly some museums will allow you to photograph details of their large-scale display models, though it is vital to check that photography is allowed as in some museums such activities are prohibited.

To conclude let me mention how useful specialist magazines can be as a source of research. In Britain there are at least three of great interest—*Model Boats, Ships Monthly* and *Sea Breezes*. These also offer back numbers if there happens to be an article you may have missed, but all are devoted to ships of all kinds and often have drawings and articles on sailing ships of interest to ship-in-bottle modellers.

Chapter 2

Useful hints

For ships in bottles

Before we proceed to look at some more complicated models it is, I think, worth considering some of the finer points of the art of putting ships in bottles. Being a staunch believer in the old adage that 'If something is worth doing it's worth doing well', I would advise the modeller planning to make a really detailed replica to purchase a set of plans of the ship of his choice from Messrs Bassett-Lowke Ltd, 18-25 Kingswell Street, Northampton. This firm markets the whole range of sailing ship plans compiled by Harold A. Underhill AMIES, the acknowledged authority on the subject. If possible buy the book he wrote, *Sailing Ship Rigs and Rigging,* a really excellent publication with completely accurate and informative accounts and illustrations of a large range of ships. The Underhill plans (and those from the book) can be scaled down easily enough and you then have the satisfaction that no one will be able to fault your work as to proportion and rigging if you stick to these plans. Another source of plans (those by David McGregor) is Neptune Models Ltd, Langton Priory, Portsmouth Road, Guildford, Surrey, GU2 5EH. (In America they are available through P. C. Coker III, Box 124, Charleston, South Carolina.)

Do not make the mistake, however, of trying to put in too much detail on a small model, as a deck soon begins to look cluttered up on a scale such as is necessary for a bottle model. A photograph the same size as your intended model is a good guide—what you can't see leave out. Of course, one can be permitted a certain degree of artistic licence as the modeller will realise that masts and yards have necessarily to be over-scale to withstand several holes being drilled in them. Similarly, to avoid that top heavy look also simplify the rigging.

Finish is, to my mind, one of the prerequisites in models of this kind and on occasion I have used anything from between 12 and 15 coats of *thin* enamel, each rubbed down with wet and dry paper as used by car body finishers. This extra work pays dividends and gives a flawless glass-like finish which makes a world of difference to your model. If desired it can be further enhanced by a *thin* coat of varnish. You can also apply a coat of clear varnish to the decks, giving them that 'wet' look as if the sea had recently swept over them, as it frequently did! Remember, though, that each coat of enamel slightly increases the width of the hull so it must be necessarily that much narrower to allow it to pass through the bottle neck without marking.

To make a first-class job of the hull it is worth the extra trouble to make a minute groove about $1/16$ in, below, and parallel to, the sheerline with the small waterline marker tool described in Chapter 1 (fig 4) and also one at the waterline $\frac{1}{16}$ in above the base of your model. Cut two threads (white Sylko is ideal) about 2½ times the length of your model, coat thinly with glue and press the thread into the grove with the round side of a pencil. Repeat this at the water- line, leaving the ends of the threads so that they can be removed just before the final coat of varnish, peeling them off gently. The cotton threads are used as a guide for your painting and are removed only when the 'boot topping' (the black finish at the sheerline down to the first thread) and the rust-red anti- fouling colour below the waterline are completed.

Choice of the mid-section colour is up to the modeller. Some clippers were brown, others dark green, some maroon, some mid-grey with a merest sugges- tion of pink. So, after the final coat of enamel, replace these threads with new white ones, stick them firmly in place and trim off the ends so that the joints cannot be seen. It is a good idea to end these right at the stern of the model, then apply your final coat of varnish and leave for about a week to harden thorough- ly. When handling the model it is advisable to hold it between finger and thumb on the deck and base of the ship. This will prevent unsightly marking of the hull finish with your fingerprints.

Masts are best made from $\frac{1}{16}$ in beech dowelling (as mentioned in Chapter 3) or cocktail sticks of the same type of fine grain wood rubbed down and tapered slightly at the top section. Masts always look much more effective when made in two or three sections (depending on the model) as shown in fig 15, Chapter 6. This was the usual sailing ship practice for square rigged vessels, except in the later days of sail when sometimes the lower and topmasts were a single 'tube' formed, of course, by steel plates. However, for a clipper ship the lower, top- mast and topgallant masts should be made as described, for as well as being technically more accurate they are also stronger, as the holes are drilled at these points for the shrouds and backstays.

When making the hull, take care that it does not occupy more than half the diameter of the bottle neck. Here we can, if necessary, use a little of that artistic licence, making the hull slightly more curved in section than an actual ship would be so that it conforms to the shape of the bottle neck. The bows, of course, can occupy three-quarters or more of the bottle neck because then the bulk of the hull, rigging, yards and sails are already partly in the bottle. This leaves only the bows, bowsprit and Dolphin Striker to go through, together with the threads that control the standing and running rigging used to erect the masts and square off the yards and to haul the spanker sail taut.

For other bottle models

The main axiom is to make *everything* first before putting *anything* in the bottle, to check constantly for size and to make sure that all dowels have a corresponding hole in the component to which they will eventually be fitted. Also, never try to do too much at one time and always allow the adhesive to dry out thoroughly before adding the next component. In later chapters of this book you will see how relatively large objects, some several times the width of the bottle neck, can be put in a bottle with only a little extra amount of ingenuity and planning. Items such as wheels, may be twice the diameter of the bottle neck, can be made by cutting the wheel in half and fixing a 'hinge' of masking tape on to the side which will not be showing. The wheel is slipped in to the bottle in its folded state then opened out flat using the side of the bottle; a little adhesive is added and then it is pressed on to the base of the bottle until set. In every instance slow-drying adhesives are better by far, such as the latex-based ones, for these give the modeller time to locate the component into the exact position desired. It will be obvious to the reader then, that the quick-drying 'contact-type' glues are taboo for this particular craft, however useful they may be for other types of model-making. A bottle modeller should always have a few wads of cotton wool on the end of stout wires at hand as these are essential to wipe away any glue smears from the bottle before they dry. Even the most experienced modeller gets the odd glue or paint smear in the bottle neck region and the quicker these are removed the better. (Paint smears can be wiped off, by using cotton wool dampened with turpentine or cellulose thinners.)

The desire to get moving straight away on a model is quite understandable but by exercising a little patience and by first studying instructions carefully the novice can save himself a whole lot of headaches and pitfalls. Experience is the best teacher of course, and there is no substitute for it, but the modeller can be spared a lot of frustration by helpful hints at the beginning and these can also be a great time saver. As soon as the modeller completes his first model he will be eager to attempt something a little more complicated. It is always worth looking through magazines or furniture catalogues, for not only can they be a source of ideas but there are often miniature reproductions of pictures, wallpaper etc, that can be incorporated in a model to give it authenticity. Mirrors can be made from metallic foil and defunct lady's wrist watch, the smaller the better, can be made into any type of clock. A fire can be represented by gold and red foil paper with tiny fragments of coal at the base while the tapered end of a ball point pen, when cut off and filed to shape, can soon be converted into a goblet or vase and the plastic ink tube of the pen can be made to represent a fluorescent light when cleaned out and painted inside. Fittings, such as chair and table legs, can be made from beech cocktail sticks and turned on an electric drill with the aid of a thin file and fine glass paper. Windows can be portrayed by means of a frame cut out from thin card, such as Bristol board, and if the modeller is good at miniature painting an outdoor scene can be incorporated to give a further realistic air. Small curtains could also be made from scraps of fine fabric. Anyone who has a flair for making small animals carved from wood could add a dog or cat or perhaps even a parrot on a perch, while small electric light bulbs can be purchased at any good class model railway shop. However, a good rule of thumb is to refrain from putting *too* much detail into a bottle model as this tends to detract from the main theme.

The bottle

By now the reader will be eager to make a start on a model and the first step is to choose the right sort of bottle for your project. Where better to find the bottle of your choice than in a wine store, or better still an alibi is now readily available if you feel like a visit to your local hostelry, where a diverse array of bottles will surely gladden the eye. Invariably inns and hotels have a batch of 'empties' in the cellar or at the back of the premises which they will be glad to get rid of as most wine, liqueur and spirit bottles are in the 'non-returnable' category. So, if you approach the proprietor at a not too busy moment he may come up with something really attractive for you. Whether the reader opts for a clear glass bottle or one of those delicately tinted green, pink or brown ones of Spanish, French or German origin the choice of a bottle is purely a matter of individual taste. However, there are a few points to watch out for. Bottles with glass lettering or embossed badges in the glass should be avoided, as should those with sharp corners or prominent seams, for any type of flaw can mar or warp the appearance of the model or models inside.

Even some of the best bottles have minor faults but, by being discerning, the best can easily be chosen for the particular model you have in mind. For instance, if the reader decides on the upright standing figure of the fisherman holding a model of a schooner in his hands (see Chapter 12), a rather obvious seam in the bottle could be effectively covered by a coat of white or very pale blue satin finish paint on the inside of the bottle; thereby serving the dual purpose of covering the defect and providing a light background to enhance the appearance and craftwork of the model.

A good round pint rum or whisky bottle, or a square Johnnie Walker whisky bottle is ideal, the latter especially so for scenic models with a harbour background. With a long bottle, incidentally, remember to make the controlling rigging longer than for a dimple bottle.

Dimple bottles are attractive and easier to work in than long square bottles, as the very shape, with concave sides, help to hold a model securely. The disadvantage is that concave curves tend to 'warp' the appearance of the model inside, a trick of light refraction, of course.

Generally speaking, the longer the bottle the more difficult it is to work in, as each movement with a handling rod or wire at the bottle neck becomes much greater at the far end. Thus a steady hand is a great asset, especially with these long bottles.

Chianti bottles, providing they have a spherical base, can also be used and the large size (pint or over) can be made to look good, particularly if mounted on a long stand. The back end of the stand needs to support the bottle at its largest circumference and the front end supports the neck of the bottle.

To ascertain the inside height of a bottle, measure the outside height or diameter and cut a piece of postcard to this shape but 1/4 in less in height, folding the card lengthways and across the centre (fig 7). Make a small hole in the centre and place it on a long 1/8 in wire about 1/4 in from the end. Secure with an elastic band, inserting it in the bottle with the ends pointing towards you. The card will straighten out inside the bottle. If it doesn't work, withdraw the card template and trim it off until the card will straighten out in the bottle. It is a wise precaution to test the *whole* length of a long bottle as sometimes the glass varies in thickness. Allow 1/2 in clearance for sea and rigging threads beneath the hull. When your masts are stepped, and before rigging, check your model for height by raising the masts separately with a piece of wire, only placing your model lightly on the sea to avoid marking the hull.

An alternative method, for measuring long pint, quart or litre bottles is to tie a thread to the centre of a cocktail stick, lower this into the bottle and keep trimming off a little wood from each end until the stick fits the diameter exactly, all the way down the bottle.

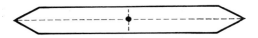

Fig 7: *Folded card template, which is secured to a length of wire by an elastic band to ascertain the interior height of long bottles.*

The next step is to clean the bottle thoroughly inside. If it is badly stained run hot water slowly into the bottle but do no rush this operation, especially if the bottle is an old one or you may crack it. Then put in a few drops of Domestos or other bleaching agent, fill the bottle and allow it to stand for at least 24 hours. This treatment should remove most stains, but if any still persist, tie a small ball of cotton wool or bandage round a stout wire and rub away the stains whilst the bottle is still full of the bleach solution. Rinse well with fresh water. If you want to make doubly sure your bottle is clean, dry the bottle out by inverting it and then shake some surgical spirit round the inside; this will give an added shine to the glass. Then invert the bottle again and allow to drain dry on a sheet of absorbent paper.

Whilst the bottle is drying you can prepare a scale drawing of the model to be made, within the scope of the internal measurement of the bottle of course! Although ideally these models would be an exact fit this is not always practicable. So, to be on the safe side, permit no less than a $^1/_{16}$ in allowance all round to give a clear margin for the slight increase in size from the layers of paint and/or glue at the base of the model. This allowance may not sound completely necessary, but in fact a few coats of paint, varnish or glue does increase the size of components more than is realised. Be certain to make every component exactly to size and work to your drawing throughout. Joints in figures, boxes or any other object to be made-up inside the bottle must be as accurate as you can possibly make them, and those parts of components to be dowelled or glued together later on must be kept free of paint. Nothing looks worse or destroys the illusion of a figure more than gaps in the joints, so with a little extra care these joints can be made almost invisible. Remember that it is virtually impossible to paint over these joints when a figure is *in situ*, but by being meticulous in your workmanship this situation should never arise.

A round bottle will need a wood stand and this, when cut out, sanded and stained or polished can make a ship model look very attractive. Place the base of your bottle on the wood selected—hard wood again—and draw the curve. Make the curve of the stand quite shallow, otherwise the sides will obstruct the view of the model. A half-inch depth is ample. Cut from a piece of wood $^3/_4$ in in section with a fretsaw and cut lengthways. This gives the two portions of the stand an identical size and shape. Join with two $^3/_{16}$ in or $^1/_4$ in dowels. Hold a sheet of sandpaper tightly around your chosen bottle and rub the stand parts down until they are a snug fit to the curve of the bottle. This is really just a simple carpentry job.

Top right *Progressive stages in the carving of the hull from the solid.*

Centre right and bottom right *Two views of the hull carved and drilled, with the inside of the bulwarks painted white, before tidying up at deck level. It is now ready for painting and varnishing.*

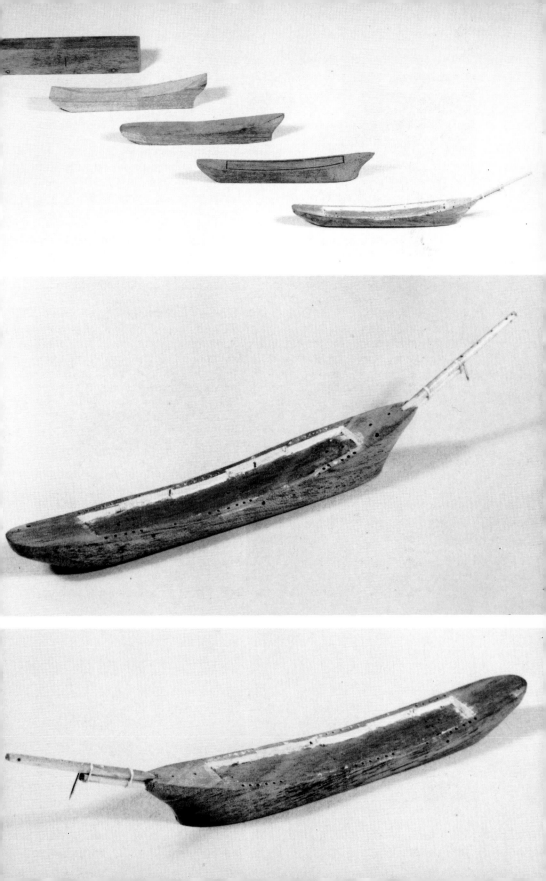

Stepping the mizzen mast, with the mainmast in position and the mast hinge clearly visible.

Commencing rigging in the shrouds, holding the foremast at the correct angle whilst threading the shrouds and backstays.

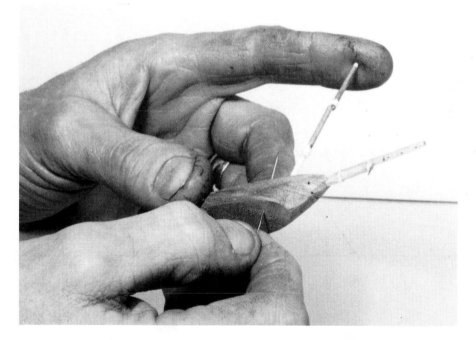

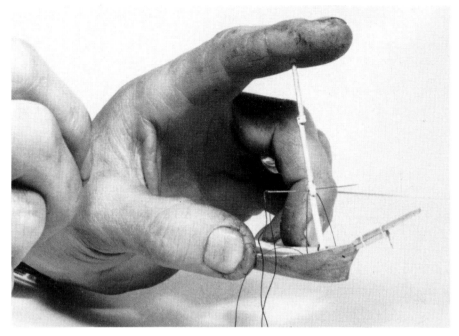

The first shroud completed and the second being threaded through the foremast doublings.

The royal backstay being threaded through the hole in the mast truck.

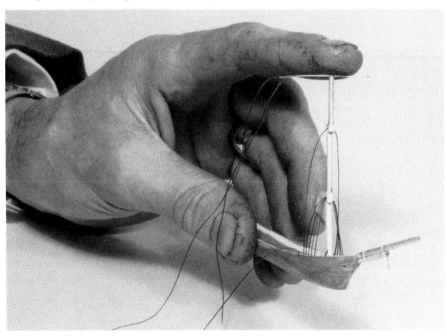

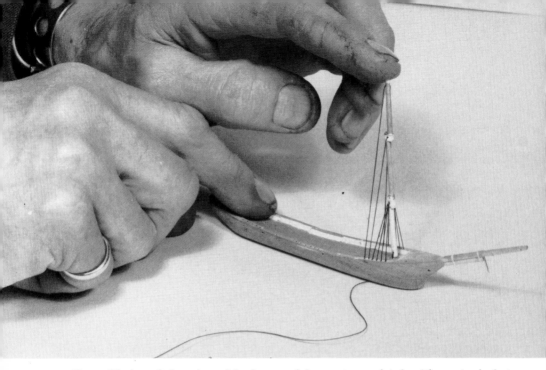

Above *Rigging of shrouds and backstays of foremast completed, with mast raked at correct angle.*

Below *Final tying of shrouds and backstays beneath the hull. Any slackness which may have developed during rigging should be drawn taut, knotted and glued.*

Above right *How the foremast collapses on its hinge.*

Right *Fore royal stay holding the foremast erect, with the fore course yard clove-hitched ready to attach to the foremast with a reef knot.*

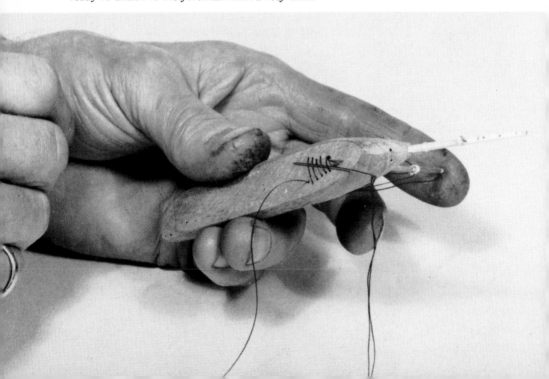

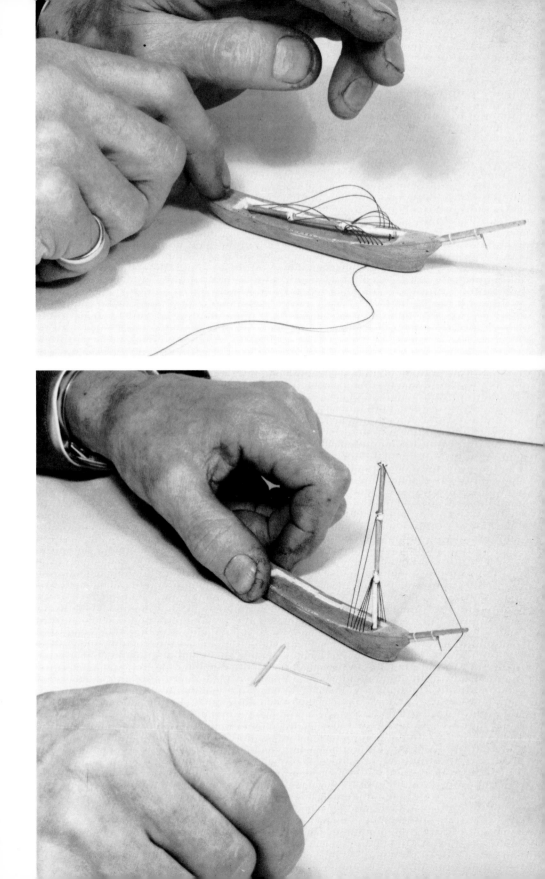

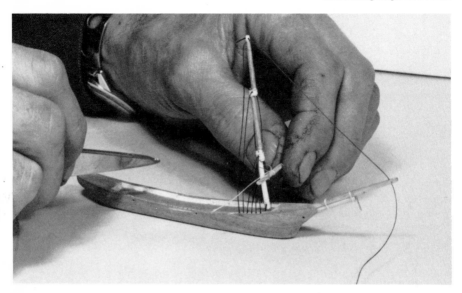

Above *Attaching the yard to the foremast. If the lower mast is painted white, use white cotton. Use fawn cotton for the yards above, to match 'stone' colour usually used for the top mast and royal mast.*

Below and above right *Two views of a clipper ship model completely rigged—square sails, staysails and jibs to be added, spanker sail in position.*

Right *The same clipper ship model, with all controlling threads clearly shown.*

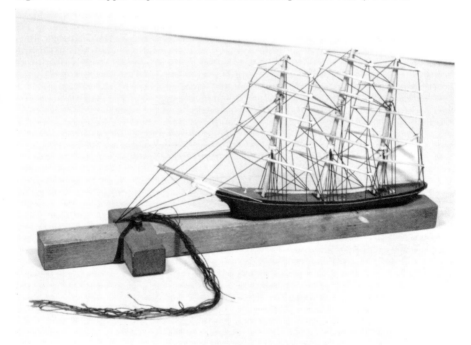

This page and right *Three more views of the clipper model, showing the masts and yards being collapsed prior to insereting the ship in its bottle. Sails are omitted here for clarity.*

Below right *A four-masted stump topgallant ('bald-headed') barque on the rigging base.*

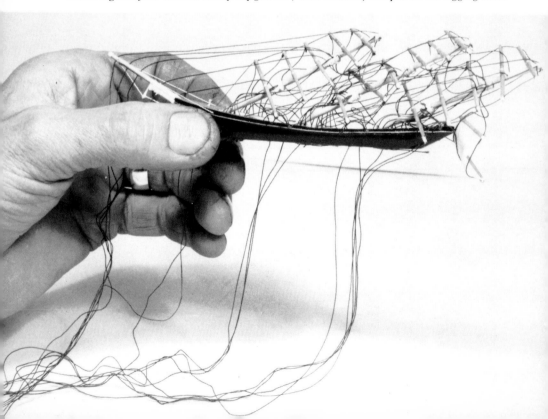

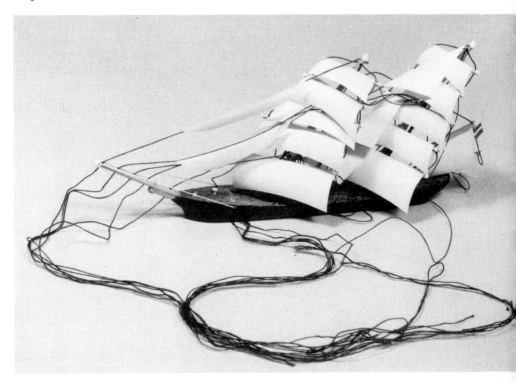

Left *A model brig shown on its wooden working stand, with rigging complete and drawn taut. In the background is the dimple bottle into which it has to fit. Also note capstan, and flag at upper gaff.*

This page *Two views of the model brig being collapsed, showing overlapping square sails and spanker sail curved to roll up for insertion into the bottle neck.*

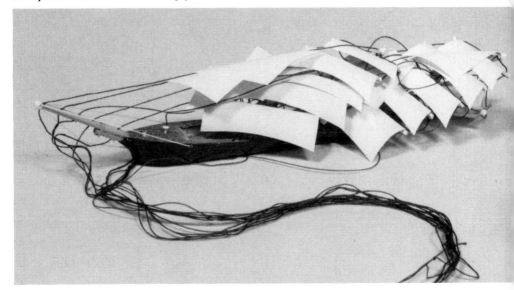

Above Gently *does it! Slowly ease the model into the bottle, keeping the spanker sail clear of the 'sea'.*

Below *Pressing the hull firmly into the 'sea', using a stout steel rod on the centre of the deck and keeping the rod clear of shrouds and backstays.*

Above right *Once the model is firmly settled, erection of masts can begin by hauling on the relevant threads. Out of apparent chaos comes order.*

Right *All hauled taut, shipshape and Bristol fashion. Secure all threads at the bottle neck with a blob of Plasticine or an elastic band, and glue the stays which pass through the bowsprit.*

Chapter 3

A simple model for the beginner

For those who have never attempted to make a ship in a bottle the model of a two-masted fore and aft schooner illustrated in fig 9 would be an ideal one to start with as there are only nine sails and no square sail yards to confuse the novice. Masts on these vessels were made very simply in two sections, lower mast and top mast, and the sections where they overlap were called crosstrees or doublings. There were literally hundreds of these coastal craft plying in trade at the beginning of the century and the example shown is typical of the type. As all the models in this book are waterline models, only this part is constructed.

The standing rigging, called shrouds and backstays, and fore and mainmast stays, which support the masts were rigged in the early days by tarred ropes and kept tight by two circular wooden blocks called 'deadeyes'. Of course, on a model of this scale they are not shown. The bottom deadeye was fastened by a metal chain plate strop to the outside of the hull. These deadeyes were used right from Elizabethan times except that then they were heart-shaped. In later days of sail, shrouds and backstays, standing rigging, etc, were set up with steel stranded wire and rigging screws.

The hull and masts of the model are made from hardwood, the former beech or mahogany and the latter beech dowelling of $\frac{1}{16}$ in diameter, obtainable from most large model shops. Select a smooth piece of wood $2\frac{1}{2}$ in long by $\frac{1}{2}$ in wide by $\frac{1}{4}$ in deep and carefully cut out the sheerline by either making a series of vertical saw cuts (see fig 8), or using a fret-saw or file. Shape the stern and bows with a file and fine glasspaper, making the bows only slightly concave, and round off stern evenly. Then shape out the plan of the hull with a craft knife and file, finishing off with fine glasspaper. Mark out the bulwarks (as shown in fig 9) with a sharp hard pencil using your second finger as a guide. Make these no less than $\frac{1}{16}$ in wide and $\frac{3}{32}$ in deep. The pencil mark is then cut with your craft knife and the deck formed by cutting the unwanted wood out with a small sharp chisel ($\frac{1}{4}$ in wide is ideal), finishing off with a folded strip of fine glass paper (wrapped over a strip of wood) until it is smooth, even and in line with the curve of the sheerline.

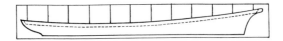

Fig 8: *A series of vertical saw cuts can assist the carving and shaping of the hull—made from a solid piece of hardwood.*

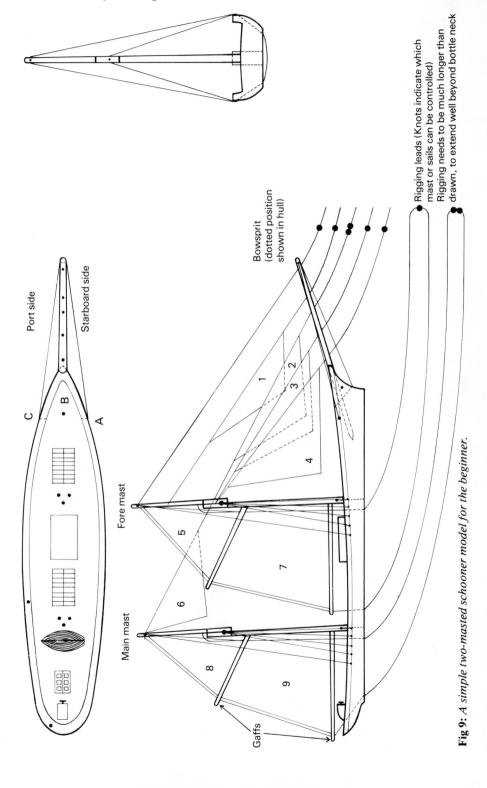

Port side

Starboard side

C B A

Fore mast

Main mast

Gaffs

Bowsprit
(dotted position
shown in hull)

1
2
3
4
5
6
7
8
9

Rigging leads (Knots indicate which
mast or sails can be controlled)
Rigging needs to be much longer than
drawn, to extend well beyond bottle neck

Fig 9: *A simple two-masted schooner model for the beginner.*

The hole is drilled for the bowsprit at the bows with a $^3/_{32}$ in drill, making sure the hole is in line with the length of the hull and following the curve of the sheer-line. Make the bowsprit hole $^1/_2$ in deep, as this has to take the strain of the mast and jib stays which hold the masts erect. The colour of the hulls of ships of this era was brown, black or dark green. Use several coats of thin enamel (Humbrol is ideal), rubbing down when each one is completely dry. Then the hull and deck can be finished off with a coat of thin varnish. Drill holes (where shown in fig 9) with a No 70 drill right through the hull, being careful to drill those in the bulwarks at an angle towards the centre of the hull, to avoid their coming out of the sides of the hull.

The holes to take the shrouds and backstays are drilled $^1/_8$ in above the water-line at an angle to bring the drill out at the bottom of the hull (see end elevation, fig 9). In writing, the construction of the hull sounds quick and simple—so it is, relatively speaking, but great care is needed at all stages, especially in symmetrical shaping and rubbing down of the hull.

The masts can now be made, tapering them towards the tops or mast trucks (to give them their proper name), securely glued and tied at the top and bottom of the doublings with clove hitches. At the foot or heel of the masts drill holes for the mast hinges, and the holes in the doublings to take the four shrouds, using a $^1/_{16}$ in drill. Holes are drilled in the truck of the mainmast, the top one being in line with the hull and the bottom one $^1/_{16}$ in below it, at 90°, i.e., across the line of the hull. This bottom hole is for the backstays. Drill holes the same in the case of the foremast and an additional one which passes through the doublings (making sure that this is above the $^1/_{16}$ in hole you have drilled for the foremast shrouds) in a fore and aft direction, or in line with the length of the hull. Make the upper and lower gaffs of $^1/_{16}$ in dowel, rubbed down smoothly, and drill a hole (No 70 drill) $^1/_{16}$ in from each end. Masts, bowsprit and gaffs should then be thinly varnished. When dry, clear the holes with your drill of any excess varnish. The bowsprit has five vertical holes and one horizontal hole at the forward end.

After fitting the bowsprit, fixing it securely and making sure the glue is dry, drill a hole (fine drill again) at point B (fig 9). Knot one end of a 12 in length of thread, which should be black cotton thread, Sylko is best, first rubbing it across a piece of beeswax to remove any fluff. Thread it to a needle and pass the needle through the deck in a downward direction, to come out at the bows, through the end hole in the bowsprit then through the two holes in the bulwarks C and A, joining the other thread at the bowsprit hole, glue and trim off the excess thread when dry. Next glue threads at the bulwark holes C and A, and when dry cut off the excess thread which crosses the deck.

To step the masts use fine wire; the thin iron wire used by florists is all right for this job. I have also used the wire out of pipe cleaners which is just the right gauge. The wire is used to hinge the masts so that they drop while the model is inserted in the bottle. This hinging of the masts is, of course, the key to the secret of ships in bottles. If you use a pipe-cleaner, just untwist the two wires, pull off the fluff and take out the kinks in the wire by pulling one end with pliers across a round steel rod, or screwdriver shank. Fig 10 shows mast fixing detail; make sure that the hinge is a snug fit at the sides of the mast and that the ends do not project below the hull. It is always as well to glue these hinges into the hull, taking care that no glue goes on the masts. To make the shrouds and backstays take an 18 in length of brown Sylko, tie a knot in the end and take the thread up-

Fig 10: *How to hinge the masts, using fine wire. The key to the secret of ships in bottles.*

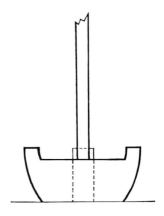

wards through the foremast hole in the hull, through the hole in the mast doublings and down through the opposite hole in the hull, repeating this for the four shrouds, then the backstays through the lower hole in the mast truck. Repeat for the mainmast.

Then cut out the sails from a good white bond paper (your local printer will sell you 15 lb or 18 lb offcuts which are ideal) curving these by rubbing a 1/8 in dowel across them. Then attach your main gaff topsail (8 in fig 9). You will observe that these gaff topsails have a cut-out portion to fit over the mast doublings. Attach the fore gaff topsail (5) in the same manner. Then glue the mainsail to the lower and upper gaffs (the holes in the gaff being vertical) and the mainsail (9) in similar fashion. To rig the mainsail take an 18 in length of brown Sylko, knot one end and thread upwards through the aftermost hole in the port side bulwark, up through the lower main gaff, then the upper gaff, up through the top hole in the mainmast truck, down through the foremast doublings and through the third hole in the bowsprit. Stand both masts erect and then thread the needle upwards through the hole in the hull just aft of the mainmast hinges. Pass the thread through the lower and upper gaffs and fasten the end at the mast doublings. Even the loop of the thread out and tie two knots in the end of the loop. When your model is in the bottle this will show you that this loop controls your second (mainmast) sails and stays.

To rig the foremast sail (7) thread the needle up through the hole in the hull at the port side bulward just forward of the mainmast, up through the gaffs as before, through the foremast truck and through the foremost hole in the bowsprit. Then up through the hole just aft of the foremast hinges, through the lower and upper gaffs, fastening at the foremast doublings. Even up the loop when mast and foresail are tight and tie one knot in the end. Take a 12 in length of Sylko, fasten it to the foremast 1/8 in below the top stay and thread it through the second hole in the bowsprit. The flying jib (1) is attached to this later. Then take an 18 in length of Sylko up through the last (5th) hole in the bowsprit, pass it through the mast doublings, even up the thread and tie tightly. After applying a small dab of glue take the thread downwards through the 4th hole in the bowsprit. The fore staysail (4) and jibs are attached afterwards.

Finally, place the model on the rigging base which was described in detail in Chapter 1. Screw down the base to your worktop and draw all rigging taut, belaying all threads around the two nails in the stand. Attach the main topmast staysail (6), but glue only the bottom half of the outer jib (2) at this stage as the masts will not fully collapse if the whole length is attached. When the model is in the bottle you can complete this glueing by means of a smear of adhesive put on to the stay with a pointed $1/16$ in dowel or wire. While your model is on its stand take the opportunity to apply small touches of glue at all gaff points and also at the mainmast truck.

This model can be put into any suitable bottle, either a flat whisky or rum type (make sure it has parallel sides, as curved ones distort the view and are no use for ship models) or a half-pint dimple bottle. Choose one with a fairly wide neck to make things easier for yourself. A more detailed consideration of bottles is given in Chapter 2.

Put in your Plasticine sea in small rolls, after making sure the bottle is clean and dry. Spread the Plasticine and press it down with the curved steel rod from your tool and gadget set. Put a tiny wafer of white Plasticine here and there on top of wave crests, saving a little for the sides of the ship, and also where the stern of the model will rest, forming the ship's wake. Plasticine is easy to work into realistic wave formations—practice on your worktop first if you've any doubts.

Having completed the sea, wipe the inside of the bottle neck and prepare to insert the model. Unscrew it from the stand, release the rigging, and roll up the foresail and mainsail, taking care to retain the curve in all sails and avoid creasing them at all costs. The mainmast will, with the mainsail and main gaff topsail, enter the bottle first. Ease in the model slowly and pull *gently* on all threads to erect the masts as your model goes into the bottle. When in place, get the steel rod, having cleaned the end thoroughly, and press the model firmly in position. Pull each thread or loop in turn until all are taut and the sails are nicely stretched. A small spot of glue is affixed at the five points on the bowsprit. Leave the model and the glue to dry out for two full days. The best way to retain tension on the rigging is to put a blob of Plasticine or an elastic band around all the threads on the outside of the bottle neck. When drying out is completed, sever all the stays where they come below the bowsprit, taking care not to cut the bowsprit stay! The other threads which come out under the hull are cut off short inside the bottle neck and the ends are hidden under the sea. In Chapter 6 there is a description of how deck fittings, boats and hatches are made and these can be added by placing them on the end of a long wire with a smear of glue underneath, quickly getting them into position before the glue sets.

The deck fittings shown on the plan of the hull are typical of those on schooners at this time. Right aft is the wheelhouse. Next is the skylight for the officer's cabin, then comes the ship's boat, hatch, deck house and hatch. As a general rule the hatches were usually painted matt black, the boat was white, and the deckhouse and wheelhouse were the same colour as the hull. Obviously, though, there were many variations in colour, as shades altered with changes in ownership.

Again leave your model for a day or two to dry out. Then glue a cork in the neck, cutting it off flush, finishing off with sealing wax or painting it with gold or any other colour to choice. A 'ship' halfpenny can be glued on if desired. Having completed this model you will doubtless wish to try a more ambitious

Right *A two-masted schooner in an enclosed stand.*

one and there are quite a few listed in this book. One rule applies to all models. Always make sure that the hull clears the sides of the bottle neck and is only half, or less, the height of the neck and, or course, leave a good clearance for the height of the masts, allowing for the sea base.

Let me stress once again that if you are a beginner make this schooner model first, don't rush it, and don't be afraid to scrap work which looks unsatisfactory. Just reading all about it here makes the work sound rather quicker than it actually is. For instance, it could take a week or more of evenings to shape and fashion the hull. There is no substitute for 'having a go', so when you've read through to the end of the book, collect your tools and materials together, come back to this chapter, and get started on the schooner model, this time working to the actual instructions. Finally let me emphasise again the need to beeswax all the thread you use before putting it on the model. The beeswax makes it waterproof, stiffens it, and obviates the fluffy appearance inherent to some degree in all thread. The beeswax is applied by holding the block of wax in one hand and pulling the thread through the edge of the block, using the gap between the two fingers as a guide. The thread cuts through the wax rather like the old style of wire cheese cutter and leaves a groove. If you've ever seen a sailmaker at work you'll already be familiar with the technique.

Chapter 4

Two schooners

A four-masted schooner for a round or square bottle

There were many four-, five-, and six-masted schooners built in America in the years between 1890 and 1902. Some were engaged in the timber or, as the Americans call it, 'lumber' trade, on inland waters like the Great Lakes, whilst others carried fir and redwood to markets in the Indian and Pacific Oceans. Many were used in the Copra trade in and amongst the South Sea Islands. They were handy vessels, combining large carrying capacity with small crews. These ships make ideal bottle models as their proportions fit a long whisky or rum bottle and are particularly suitable for the beginner who has already cut his teeth on the small schooner in Chapter 3. The fore, main, mizzen and jigger sails can be rolled up on their gaffs, as you would roll up a cigarette, so they consequently take up little room in the bottle neck. With the four jib/staysails and gaff topsails there are, in fact, only 12 sails on the model.

The four masts are made in two sections and are all the same height. The hull is carved in hardwood. When your hull is carved and the holes are drilled for rigging, put a wire hinge in an ordinary cocktail stick and insert the hinge temporarily in the holes, which will eventually accommodate the jigger mast; insert the hull with the cocktail stick lying aft and raise the stick with a hooked wire. You will find you have to trim off probably $\frac{1}{2}$ in but it is an easy matter to let your temporary mast collapse, drop out the hull and trim off the excess wood until the mast is able to reach a vertical position.

As the sides of these bottles are rarely completely parallel it is a good idea to try your temporary mast in each of the four positions, bearing in mind that, with the sheer of the hull, the main and mizzen lower masts will have to be fractionally longer so that all the mast trucks will be of uniform height. The sea your model will rest in will be approximately $\frac{1}{4}$ in deep, so remember to deduct that from the mast height. The hull should measure $4\frac{1}{2}$ in long (with the bowsprit, $5\frac{1}{4}$ in) to keep the proportions correct. A single stay is used to erect all four masts, with an 18 in length of Sylko leading from the hole right in the stern of the hull. Knot and glue this well, and trim off excess thread when completely dry. Then thread the needle through all four masts just above the doublings, glueing the stay at the doublings on the jigger mast at the correct angle. Next take this long stay through the second hole in the bowsprit. Then thread another 12 in length from the foremast truck through the first vertical hole in the bowsprit. This is the stay which carries the flying jib. Each mast is rigged with four shrouds and one backstay, the latter being taken through the hole drilled in the mast $^1/_{16}$ in below the truck.

See that all masts are parallel when rigged, and raked astern about three degrees. Each upper gaff is rigged from the mast truck by passing a 24 in length of Sylko thread through the forward end of the gaff, down through the lower gaff hole, and through the hole in the hull abaft the mast. Draw down the thread to position the sail correctly, then thread it back through the next hole aft in the port side of the bulwarks and through the after end of the lower and upper gaff holes. Then take it back to the mast truck, glueing this to the end of the thread which you began with.

Stretch the sails, leaving a slight curve just as they would appear in a breeze. This will enable you to roll up the sail prior to inserting the model when all the rigging is completed.

Note that gaff topsails are glued to the masts beforehand. Put a spot of adhesive at the four points asterisked on the gaff drawing in fig 11 so that the upper gaff is positioned almost touching the gaff topsails.

The bowsprit is rigged with a Dolphin Striker and the stays are rigged as in the case of the simple schooner model described in Chapter 3. The topmast staysail and outer and inner jib sails are then fitted on to their stays. Next, put a knot in the end of each stay which controls the foremast and four knots in the single stay which goes through all the masts. The loops formed when the fore, main, mizzen and jigger sails are added should also carry the appropriate number of knots. Always allow for at least six inches of thread to protrude from the bottle neck to facilitate control of mast erection.

A typical example of this type of schooner had large hatches for timber cargoes, one each between main and mizzen masts and between mizzen and jigger. There was also a large deckhouse abaft the foremast with two doors, three or four portholes and a thick glass skylight, which can be represented by an oblong of silver paper. A capstan on the fo'c'sle deck can be made from a large pin cut to about $^1/_4$ in long, painted grey or white and with the top $^3/_{32}$ in above the deck. Ship's boats were either stowed upturned on the deck, or one was slung from davits astern. These latter fittings are made from headless pins bent into a graceful curve, painted white and fitted into two holes drilled in the after end of the poop deck. These and the ship's boat must be fitted *before* the model is inserted into the bottle. The deckhouse was either painted green or brown, or sometimes a buff colour, or it can be made of real mahogany thinly varnished. Deck hatches were usually closed by tarpaulin-covered planks, which can best be represented in matt black.

As with all models, a thin coat of varnish to gaffs, deck, hull and masts and a $^1/_{16}$ in tip of white paint to the mast trucks and after end of gaffs, bowsprit and Dolphin Striker will show off the model to the best advantage. When all your various fittings are made the model is collapsed by rolling up the jigger gaff sail, working forward and repeating with the remaining three masts. Care must be taken not to crease any sail and the model is inserted stern first.

Of course your sea is already in position and about $^1/_4$ in deep. It needs to be fairly flat as a ship does not carry full sail in a gale-swept sea! Make sure the neck of the bottle is perfectly clean. If preferred, a wood template, the exact shape of the under section of the hull, can be pressed into the sea first, to bed the model securely in the base. This is easily withdrawn afterwards with a long bent wire, prior to inserting the model. Press the hull firmly in and hold whilst

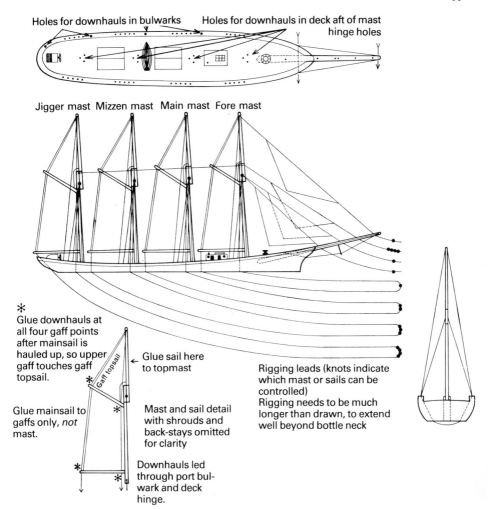

Holes for downhauls in bulwarks **Holes for downhauls in deck aft of mast**
hinge holes

Jigger mast Mizzen mast Main mast Fore mast

*
Glue downhauls at
all four gaff points
after mainsail is
hauled up, so upper
gaff touches gaff
topsail.

Gaff topsail

← Glue sail here
to topmast

Glue mainsail to
gaffs only, *not*
mast.

Mast and sail detail
with shrouds and
back-stays omitted
for clarity

Downhauls led
through port bul-
wark and deck
hinge.

Rigging leads (knots indicate
which mast or sails can be
controlled)
Rigging needs to be much
longer than drawn, to extend
well beyond bottle neck

Fig 11: *A four-masted schooner.*

the masts are erected, at which stage the Plasticine sea can be pressed into slight waves along each side of the hull, putting a couple of white waves just past the bows. These waves help to hold the model when the rigging is drawn taut.

To keep the main and mizzen masts parallel apply a minute quantity of Duro-fix or similar rapid-drying adhesive where the single stay passes through the main and mizzen mast doublings, holding the masts until the adhesive dries. When all is drawn completely taut, put a blob of Plasticine over the rigging which protrudes from the bottle neck, and add adhesive at the points where the jib stays come through the bowsprit. The excess rigging is then cut off as previously described.

Finally, deck fittings are affixed with Copydex, which dries slowly and gives ample time to get them placed correctly before setting. As usual, give it all a few days to dry out, cork firmly, finishing with sealing wax or paint, and either tie a

Turk's Head around the bottle neck or glue a 'ship' halfpenny to the cork which is cut off flush with the end of the bottle neck.

These schooners, though not highly detailed, can look very attractive. The rigging drawing (fig 11) shows a typical four-masted schooner, not based on a particular prototype but thoroughly representative of the breed. The instructions given here are not so highly detailed on specific points as they are in Chapter 3. This is simply because the four-master is only really an enlarged version of the little two-master and all that I've said on making the simpler model applies equally, of course, to the four-master.

The *Charlotte Rhodes*

One of the most popular television series for over a decade was *The Onedin Line,* with its haunting theme music from *Spartacus* by the Russian composer Khachaturyan. Almost instantly the series had an audience of 12 million which increased rapidly as the series was sold abroad. Although the series featured many well-known actors, the undisputed 'star' was the three-masted topsail schooner *Charlotte Rhodes,* which many people on holiday around Dartmouth harbour saw whilst being filmed. Originally built in Denmark in 1904 as the *Eva,* then re-named the *Meta Jan,* she was owned in the late 1960s by Captain J. Macreth, who again changed her name. The actual harbour location used for the first sequences of *The Onedin Line* was, in fact, Bayards Cove, a quaint cobbled quay steeped in history. It was from here that Richard the Lion Heart and his crusaders left for Messina in 1190. Sir Walter Raleigh was a frequent visitor in the 16th century and, in 1620, the *Mayflower* was moored nearby while waiting for the *Speedwell* to be repaired. This cove proved an ideal location for the series and by removing some TV masts and 'No Parking' signs a 19th century 'Liverpool' was created. Unfortunately someone left an electric light bulb in one of the street lamps which were rather rare in the mid-19th century. However, apart from that *faux pas,* the series was excellent.

Unfortunately the *Charlotte Rhodes* is no longer with us, as after being sold to a Dutchman, there was a mysterious explosion on board the ship in Holland and she was totally destroyed by fire. However, this vessel does make an ideal subject for a model in a 1 pint dimple bottle and, with her distinctive red-brown sails and white bulwarks above a black hull, looks most attractive. She is not a difficult ship to model either, when compared with the five-masted square rigged ship *Preussen* or the seven-masted schooner *Thomas W. Lawson.* A model I made of the *Charlotte Rhodes* was exhibited at both Fort Balaguier and Cannes in 1979 and a miniature model of the ship in a penicillin bottle 2 in × ⁷⁄₈ in was also made at this time. Actually, one of the hardest tasks with these models was getting the correct colour paper for the sails, for it is a rather distinctive shade and very different from the Thames sailing barges who had sails of a definite brown. Her hull is painted black with white bulwarks and a white line follows the 'sheer' of the hull. The masts and gaffs are a buff/stone colour (Humbrol HR 112 paint) which was a typical mast colour in that era. The ship usually flew the 'red duster' from the upper gaff and for the TV series, the Onedin house flag, a white 'O' with a white line beneath on a blue background. The *Charlotte Rhodes* had a wooden covered structure right in the forepeak into which the bowsprit fitted and further aft a windlass (which I made from sheet metal and watch parts) and aft of this was a companion-way hatch leading to

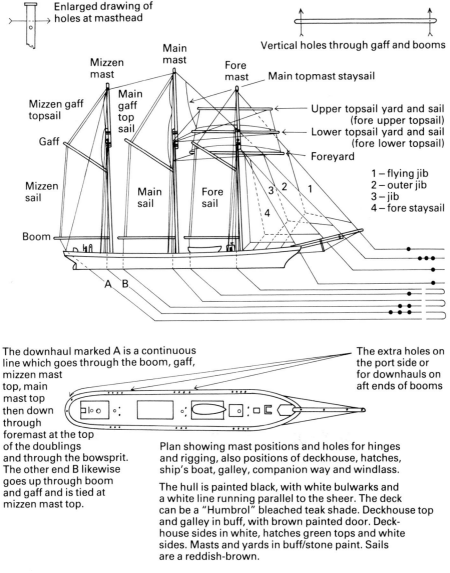

Enlarged drawing of holes at masthead

Vertical holes through gaff and booms

Mizzen mast

Main mast

Fore mast

Mizzen gaff topsail

Main gaff top sail

Main topmast staysail

Gaff

Upper topsail yard and sail (fore upper topsail)

Lower topsail yard and sail (fore lower topsail)

Foreyard

Mizzen sail

Main sail

Fore sail

1 – flying jib
2 – outer jib
3 – jib
4 – fore staysail

Boom

A B

The downhaul marked A is a continuous line which goes through the boom, gaff, mizzen mast top, main mast top then down through foremast at the top of the doublings and through the bowsprit. The other end B likewise goes up through boom and gaff and is tied at mizzen mast top.

The extra holes on the port side or for downhauls on aft ends of booms

Plan showing mast positions and holes for hinges and rigging, also positions of deckhouse, hatches, ship's boat, galley, companion way and windlass.

The hull is painted black, with white bulwarks and a white line running parallel to the sheer. The deck can be a "Humbrol" bleached teak shade. Deckhouse top and galley in buff, with brown painted door. Deckhouse sides in white, hatches green tops and white sides. Masts and yards in buff/stone paint. Sails are a reddish-brown.

Fig 12: *The* Charlotte Rhodes, *'star' of* The Onedin Line; *a three-masted topsail schooner with distinctive red/brown sails.*

the crews' quarters in the forecastle. Immediately aft of the foremast was the galley, complete with cowled chimney and door, then came the forrard hatch, with green canvas cover and white sides, above which was the ship's boat on chocks. I have seen the ship's boat mounted both athwartships and fore and aft, so this can be put in either position. The ship's pumps were situated immediately aft of the mainmast next to the after cargo hatch. The after deck-house was immediately aft of the mizzen mast and this had a companion way leading to the saloon right at the after end. On top of the deckhouse were the ship's helm

The Charlotte Rhodes *in a dimple bottle.*

(wheel) and forrard of that the binnacle. The last time I saw the ship in Dartmouth she had a rather ugly rail around the deckhouse, a rather incongruous modern structure made of galvanised pipe, which I tactfully omitted in the model. There is a model of this ship in a ½ pint dimple Haig bottle which I presented to the Butterwalk Museum a few years ago. This model should not present any problems at all and a drawing of the ship giving details of size and colours is given below.

Chapter 5

The *Waterwitch*

This famous three-masted wood barquentine was one of the best known vessels amongst sailormen in the West of England. Although built more than 100 years ago by Meadus of Poole (she was originally a brig with raised quarter deck and grossed 207 tons), she is still remembered with great affection. Unfortunately her deep draught was rather a disadvantage in the coastal trade, but she made some fast deep sea voyages in the fruit and fish trade. Like the fictional Captain Ahab in Herman Melville's book *Moby Dick* which featured the adventures of the whaling ship *Pequod,* one of the *Waterwitch*'s captains actually *did* have a wooden leg and had holes drilled in the after deck to give him a secure foothold (if that's the correct term!) at sea. In the First World War she lay sunk in Newlyn Harbour for almost four years, then afterwards was refloated and partially rebuilt. She spent many years in the Cornish china clay trade, as did many West Country schooners, and was owned by Mr Stephens of Fowey, Cornwall. Many Trinity House pilots did their sea service in this fine old barquentine to qualify for their certificates.

This ship, with a little simplification of rigging, can be a fine subject for a dimple bottle model, half-pint size (see fig 13). Only the position of the mainmast stay sail (5 on the diagram) has been altered to simplify rigging. This model serves to introduce us to the added complication of crossed yards, all on the foremast. Start by selecting a suitably sized block of hardwood and draw out, carve and sand the hull to shape, as described earlier.

Drill the hole for the bowsprit with a $^3/_{32}$ in drill, making sure that it is in line with the fore and aft line of the hull. The hole should be $^1/_2$ in deep and at an angle to follow the sheerline. The bowsprit is made from $^1/_{16}$ in dowel, tapered to the forward end and $1^1/_8$ in long. There should be $^7/_8$ in projecting from the bows, and it should be drilled with five vertical holes and one horizontal hole $^1/_{16}$ in from the end.

As fig 13 shows, the shrouds and backstays on *Waterwitch* were rigged on the outside of the hull and the hull has to be a trifle narrower than scale to pass through into the bottle. So the holes for this standing rigging must be drilled just above the waterline and at an angle to bring the rigging underneath the hull. This is the safest way of doing things, as if you drill right through the hull horizontally you always come out the other side in the wrong place. Use a No 70 drill and keep the holes as close together as possible, being careful not to let them run in to each other.

Masts are made in sections, as can be seen in the diagram, of $^1/_{16}$ in dowel or

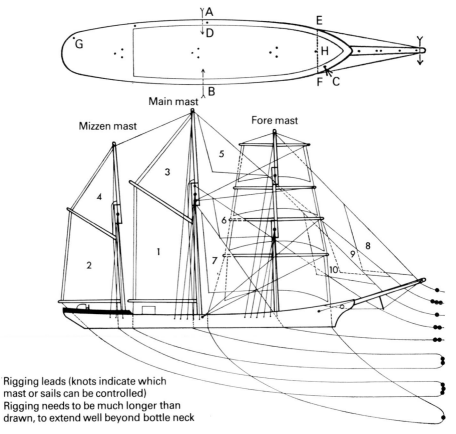

Main mast

Mizzen mast   Fore mast

Rigging leads (knots indicate which
mast or sails can be controlled)
Rigging needs to be much longer than
drawn, to extend well beyond bottle neck

Fig 13: Waterwitch—*a three-masted barquentine. (Port braces not shown for sake of clarity.)*

beech cocktail sticks sanded down and tapering towards the top. Join them at the doublings with glue and clove hitches. Holes must be drilled at the foot of each mast for the wire hinges. Fairly large holes are needed in the middle of the doublings as these have to accommodate five threads (shrouds) in the case of the mainmast, four in the foremast and three in the mizzen. Also holes are drilled in all the mast trucks, two in the mainmast, and two in the foremast, the former to accommodate backstays and the stay which comes in one continuous length from the hole (G) right in the stern of the hull. So one hole, the lower one, is drilled at an angle of 90° to the fore and aft line of the hull and the top hole is in line with the hull.

Holes are drilled in a fore and aft direction for the stays to pass through from the mainmast to the foremast and through the bowsprit. Remember to make all rigging leads long enough to pass well clear, at least 5 in from the bottle neck and rub each length of Sylko (either brown or black) through beeswax to remove any furriness. The rigging leads from all masts are clearly shown in fig 13, as are the flying, outer, inner jibs and forestay sail.

The attaching of the square sails on the foremast is the same for that used on all square-rigged models. The yards are round in section, tapering towards each end, and drilled (No 70 drill) $1/16$ in from each end and tied dead centre to the mast. Always apply adhesive on knots as soon as you tie them, trimming off the ends when the glue is dry. The main gaff topsail (3) is glued to the mast at its longest edge. Similarly, the mizzen gaff topsail (4) is attached to the mizzen mast. The main (1) and mizzen sails (2) are curved by rolling a $1/8$ in dowel across them. They are then securely glued to their respective upper and lower gaffs, these being round and tapered towards each end and drilled as were the square sail yards. I find it better to thinly varnish all masts, gaffs and bowsprits.

Take a length of Sylko 24 in long, thread it upwards through the aftermost hole in the hull, then take it through the after hole in the lower mizzen gaff, through the upper gaff, then through the hole in the foretop mast doubling and through the third hole in the bowsprit. The other end of the thread goes up through the hole in the hull just aft of the mizzen mast, through the forward ends of the lower and upper gaffs, and the end is secured at the mast doublings. Even up the thread ends after trying all mast hinges, put a spot of adhesive at the mizzen mast truck and tie three knots in the two ends of the threads. This will indicate that these actuate your third or mizzen mast.

Then take another 24 in length of Sylko, thread through the hole in the hull immediately forward of the mizzen mast (on the port side of bulwarks), up through the gaffs as before, but this time fastening at the mainmast truck. If preferred, instead of tying knots at these points use a 'Lazy Splice', ie, push the needle back through the thread, draw tight and glue. This method is actually neater than knots. The other end of the thread is taken up through the hole in the hull, immediately aft of the mainmast, and fastened at the mast doublings. Even up the thread ends and tie two knots in the end to indicate that they actuate the second or mainmast. Now is the best time to screw your hull on to its stand whilst completing the rigging and attaching the staysails, jibs and square sails. Draw all threads taut and belay round the two nails at the end of the stand like a figure of eight. Then loop a small elastic band over the threads as an extra precaution against the rigging slackening. Apply adhesive at the four gaff holes on mizzen and mainsails when stretched to a nice curve. Having evened up the masts, which should cant back to about 88° you can now attach the main top gallant staysail (5), the main topmast staysail (6) and the main staysail (7). Take a 12 in length of Sylko and fasten to the foremast truck and thread through the foremost hole in the bowsprit, tying one knot in the end, then glue on the flying jib (8). The outer jib stay is another 12 in length of Sylko attached to the doublings above the fore upper topsail and taken through the second hole in the bowsprit, tying one knot in the end as an indicator. Then attach the outer jib sail.

The fore topmast staysail and forestay sail are attached to the stays but only glue the bottom half for the time being, otherwise the masts will not fold back. When the model is in the bottle with masts erected and main and mizzen sails stretched the top half of these two sails can be secured by putting a smear of adhesive on the stays with a pointed $1/16$ in dowel or wire and pressing the tops of the sails firmly down. The four square sails are attached in the same way as outlined in Chapter 6. Then take a 24 in length of Sylko up through the hole in the starboard side of the deck near the bowsprit (C), thread it up through the four yards, then through the foremast truck and down through the opposite ends of the yards, and finally down through the hole in the port side of the deck (D). Even up the threads and this time tie one knot in the ends.

The bowsprit is then rigged as follows. Cut a pin head off leaving the pin $5/32$ in long and glue into the hole in the bowsprit. This is known as a martingale or, more commonly, the 'Dolphin Striker'. Thinly paint this brown. When dry, thread a 12 in length of black Sylko down through hole H in the fo'c'sle deck which comes out through the bows. Take a round turn round the bottom end of the Dolphin Striker, glue and take through the horizontal hole at the forward end of the bowsprit. Then lead it through the bulwarks on the port side at E across the deck, out through hole F opposite and back to the bowsprit end. Glue it after knotting on to the vertical thread leading from the Dolphin Striker. Glue threads at each side of the bulwarks, and when dry cut off the excess thread which lies across the deck.

Braces (which lead from the ends of the yards to the deck and mainmast) for the forecourse, the bottom square sail yard, are taken through hole A in the bulwarks, across the deck and out at B back to the yards. Make certain these threads do not pass through the existing threads at the yard ends, but pass freely through the holes in the yards. This is *most important* to ensure that the yards swivel easily when the masts are folded before placing the ship in the bottle. The same procedure is taken on the fore lower topsail and the braces for the fore upper topsail are taken through the hole at the bottom of the mainmast doublings and those for the fore lower top gallant are taken through the hole at the top of the mainmast doublings. Check all four braces to see that they are uniformly taut. Square off all yards and glue braces at each side of A and B cutting off when dry any excess threads which cross the deck.

Unscrew the model from the base and free your controlling threads. Then curl the mizzen sail and main sails as you would roll a cigarette. Tilt the square sails and overlap them, the forecourse being overlapped by the fore lower topsail and so on. Avoid creasing or folding the sails at all costs, keeping the curve in all sails as you fold up your model. Gently ease the model stern first into the bottle, having first made sure that the inside of the neck is perfectly clean. You will find the mizzen mast and sails enter the bottle before the bulk of the hull. Be careful that this mast and its sails do not touch the sea as you do this. When your model is in the bottle, and all threads are running clear through the bottle neck, press the hull gently into the sea with the stout steel rod described in Chapter 1. Check that all is well, then pull gently on the thread you rigged first, ie, the one which comes through the third hole in the bowsprit and which has three indicating knots. Then gently erect all masts by means of the single strands of thread—and *gently* is the watchword! The foremast sails are squared off by the looped rigging, pulling one thread at a time. When completed pull down the mizzen and main sails.

Tighten all rigging, temporarily fastening all single threads outside the bottle by placing a blob of Plasticine over these and pressing all firmly to the glass. Then cut off all looped threads from the mizzen main and foremast and 'bury' these threads under the sea, if necessary covering with a wafer thin patch of Plasticine. Apply adhesive sparingly to the four stays which come through the bowsprit. Leave the glue two days to dry out. Put a little piece of muslin over the bottle neck, meanwhile, as this keeps out dust. After this drying-out process, cut off the ends of all stays which come through the bowsprit, being careful not to sever the bowsprit stays. The tool for this job is described in Chapter 1 among the other gadgets.

Add a few wafer thin wisps of white Plasticine at intervals along both sides of the hull, merging the white slightly into the blue Plasticine and add the tiniest fragments of white to wave crests and bow waves. The preparation of bottles and the placing of the Plasticine and white wake at the stern of the ship is dealt with in Chapters 3 and 4.

When your model is dried out and firmly in the bottle, the deck house, wheelhouse and companion way, davits, hatches, etc, can be added. As stated earlier in this chapter, *Waterwitch* had a raised quarter deck, on which were a curved top panelled wheelhouse, a skylight and a small chimney from the stove in the living quarters. There was also a water tank on the starboard side just forward of the quarter deck, and a boat on davits on the portside between the main and mizzen masts. Just aft of the foremast was a fairly large deck house. These fittings can be quite easily made from small pieces of hardwood. A small toothed wheel from the mechanism of a wrist-watch makes an ideal wheel. Davits are made from bent headless pins, the chimney is made from a short thick pin, and skylights are cut from tiny pieces of silver paper. Paint these deck fittings brown and thinly varnish them. To put them into position, use a long thin wire or bicycle spoke flattened at the end to form a small platform. Put a dab of adhesive under each fitting, place it upside down on the platform and position it as near as possible to the correct location, moving subsequently to correct the location quickly before the glue or adhesive sets. A magnetised wire is a good way of placing davits in the ship, pressing them firmly down into their respective holes after lightly glueing the bottom ends.

To finish off your model, when it is completely dried out and all glue marks are wiped off with a damp wad of cotton wool bound on to a wire, glue a cork in the bottle neck, cutting it off flush with the end. Seal it with wax or a 'ship' half-penny as previously described. A decorative Turk's Head knot round the bottle neck is an optional adornment, for those familiar with nautical ropework.

Chapter 6

Clipper ships

Clipper ships, those most beautiful creations of man, were so called because of their remarkable passages around the Cape of Good Hope with cargoes of tea from China, and for their ability to clip days or hours off an existing record. This straight away established a captain and his ship in the public's imagination, long before the Suez and Panama Canals were dreamed of. These remarkable vessels sped on their way at up to 21 knots which, with sail, skill and back-breaking toil, was no mean achievement. For years steam ships could not hold a candle to them for sheer speed. Credit must be given to the Americans in this venture around the middle 1800s, and some years elapsed before the first English clippers came on the scene. These early American clippers were beautiful craft, many of 900 tons or less and having a crew of between 30 and 40 (a contrast to the days at the turn of the present century when the *Thomas W. Lawson*, a seven-masted schooner of 5,218 tons, was manned by only 16 men!) who could often weigh anchor and get the ship under sail in less than half-an-hour.

These 'softwood' ships (their hulls were usually constructed of pine) unfortunately had a very short life span because of the remorseless way they were driven, and the hulls soon became strained and prone to leakage. But, despite the timeless controversies which these ships and their passages have provoked amongst marine authors, they still *did* cover these distances in record time and the *James Baines* did achieve 21 knots, while 436 miles in 24 hours were covered by the *Lightning*. The British ships were constructed of much harder woods, and later composite iron and wood, consequently lasting for years and years, many ending up as coal hulks in various parts of the Southern Hemisphere. But, with the opening of the Suez Canal in 1869, the days of the tea clipper were numbered and by 1872 the end of these magnificent vessels was in sight.

It is food for thought, though, that until three years before De Lesseps completed his Canal, sail had always been faster than steam. Then, as Australia's wool export trade developed, cargoes became available and such ships as *Thermopylae* and *Cutty Sark* achieved great fame, the latter making one of her fastest passages from Sydney to England in 70 days. This ship was so remarkable that she deserves a chapter to herself. Happily she is still with us and, over 100 years old, is now fully restored and in a permanent dry dock berth at Greenwich, London.

Of course, many people who read about clipper ships get carried away by the glamour of it all. For all the joy of being the first home with a cargo and all the fame it brought to shipbuilders, captains and crews, it will be realised that there is another side to the coin. Unlike steam ships, sailing ships could not sail in direct lines or along the shortest routes. They were at the mercy of wind and weather, and a voyage of 9,000 miles for instance might be in reality nearer 12,000 because of their having to take advantage of prevailing winds (sometimes no wind at all, in the 'Doldrums') and having to tack, or wear ship, which to the layman means in simple terms to swing all the square sail yards around an angle of perhaps 80° in order to catch a breeze, however short. When one realises that the main yards of some latter-day sailing ships weighed in the region of nine tons each, it can be realised what sheer hard work this entailed, day after day, week after week, handling stiff wet canvas, often in freezing rain or snow and sometimes in pitch darkness. Most shipowners were careful to the point of being parsimonious regarding materials and heaven help a captain who had a 'suit' of sails carried away in a gale or was hindered by a crew who could not furl sail quickly enough!

Food in those days was usually of poor quality, rations were kept at an absolute minimum and often bought from a wily ship's chandler who gave out back-handers to a captain at the expense of the crews. After a few weeks such desirable commodities as potatoes, vegetables and bread had disappeared from the menu—if that's what you can call salt pork, weevil-ridden biscuits and the like. Fresh water was rationed, sometimes to half a bucketful a day for drinking, washing clothes and brewing tea. To add to this the crew were usually accommodated below the fo'c'sle, a damp, musty, dimly lit space often awash with sea water and the accumulated debris of smashed crockery and fittings which had come adrift in heavy seas. Many of the crew suffered salt water boils and serious complaints like scurvy, (a condition caused through lack of fresh fruit, vegetables and, as we know now, vitamin deficiency). There was no means of drying clothes, bedding or gloves and boots. The misery could go on for months until the ship reached warmer climates, when all the crews' pitiful collection of mildewed possessions could be brought up on to the upper deck to dry. No wonder crews used to go ashore and get drunk at the first opportunity—surely no men had a better excuse! So difficult was it in the 1800s to get crews that men were often 'Shanghaied' from some tavern ashore and awoke hours later and miles out to sea, penniless and usually with a large lump on their heads, caused by some 'Bucko' mate hitting them with a belaying pin. Waterproof and wool clothing had to be bought, often at extortionate prices from the ship's 'Slop Chest' and the unfortunate seaman at the end of a voyage as often as not had no money and was even in debt.

There was also a practice, rife in most countries, for some seamen to be approached as soon as their ship entered port, to be hailed by some 'gentleman' in a boat and piled with crude drinks and a promise of an 'easy' ship. These men, often under the misnomer of 'boarding house keepers' were traffickers in humanity, selling besotted or unconscious seamen to a captain who was a few men short because other men had deserted. Naturally some of these 'boarding house keepers' and 'crimps' met a very sticky end, for such treatment as they meted out to seamen was not an action to be easily forgotten.

As practically none of these clipper ships ever carried a doctor it was usually the captain's job to reset broken arms and legs, or to extract recalcitrant molars, and more than one seaman survived primitive operations for appendicitis. The usual 'anaesthetic' was rum or some other spirit. The mind boggles at the agony and hardship some mariners experienced in those 'good old days', yet such was the fascination of these ships that many an apprentice paid a premium to join the band of seafarers and see the world the hard way.

Life on a sailing ship did have some compensations for when a ship reached warm latitudes a seaman was given the opportunity to swim, and spend his leisure time with various hobbies such as wood carving, rugmaking or knitting (almost every sailor could knit garments) so a lot of the hardship was temporarily forgotten. Most men stayed in this calling all their lives, often because it was the only trade they knew, probably hoping one day to find an 'easy' ship where accommodation and food was good. Such vessels were very rare, however. The only interest of the shipowners was in a fast passage, an absolute minimum wastage of canvas cordage and every last copper accounted for. Many ships were uninsured—except for their cargoes!

Years elapsed before sailing ship men obtained anything like a square deal. Yet in the 1920s and 1930s many people paid to take passages on these ships and see things at first hand. Even then conditions had not greatly improved, but sail training did something for a man that steam never could. The number of countries who still run sail training vessels is a confirmation of this fact, England, America, Denmark, Sweden, Norway, Japan, Russia and Belgium to mention but a few, still believe sail training is a 'must'.

A clipper ship for a large 'dimple' bottle

The pinnacle of achievement for the ship-in-bottle maker is a fully rigged clipper of the great era of sail of 100 or so years ago. Models of this type were the old-time sailorman's special province. When you have made some of the easier models so far described you should have confidence enough for clipper ship modelling.

For the hull of a ship model of this type always use a good hard wood such as beech, teak or mahogany, possible from an old piece of furniture. This will probably have had many years of seasoning. Old well-matured hard wood is more difficult to work but the overall result will be much more satisfactory. The lines of the hull and the inside bulwarks keep sharper and hard wood takes a much better finish when enamelled and varnished. There are other considerations, too, because when holes are drilled for shrouds, backstays, mast hinges, etc, they will look neater and not distort when the rigging is tightened. The section of wood should measure $3/4$ in $\times 3/4$ in $\times 4^{1}/2$ in and a card template of the hull elevation and deck plan should first be made and the elevation marked on both sides of the wood. I am assuming, of course, that you have already chosen a prototype, have acquired scale drawings, and done as much basic research as is needed. For anyone who has not found a specific prototype, I suggest you work from the drawings which portray a typical clipper (see fig 14).

If you do not possess a fretsaw, the best way of cutting out your hull has already been shown in fig 8. Make a series of saw cuts vertically and cut off a section at a time with the chisel, filing the excess wood down until you have a smooth sheerline. Some ships had greatly curved sheerlines. An example which springs to mind is the five-masted barque *France II*. However the *Cutty Sark*'s sheer is much less pronounced, as was *Mount Stewart*'s and *Cromdale*'s. So examine your plans and/or photographs carefully before cutting out the sheer. Then mark out your deck plan and cut out the shape with saw, file, chisel and

Key to sail plan: *1 flying jib; 2 outer jib; 3 inner jib; 4 fore topmast staysail; 5 fore royal; 6 fore topgallant; 7 fore upper-topsail; 8 fore lower topsail; 9 fore course; 10 main skysail; 11 main royal; 12 main topgallant; 13 main upper topsail; 14 main lower topsail; 15 main course; 16 mizzen topgallant; 18 mizzen upper topsail; 19 mizzen lower topsail; 20 mizzen or cro'jack; 21 spanker.*

For the sake of clarity the shrouds and backstays and braces for all yards have been omitted, as have deck fittings. The fore and aft triangular sails between fore and main mast are, reading downwards, main royal staysail, main topgallant staysail and main topmast staysail. Those between main and mizzen masts are, reading downwards, miz-zen royal staysail, mizzen middle staysail and mizzen topmast staysail.

NB: Prior to 1870 the yards and sails were named differently. The rigging has been slightly modified for a bottle model, but follows as closely as possible that of an actual clipper ship.

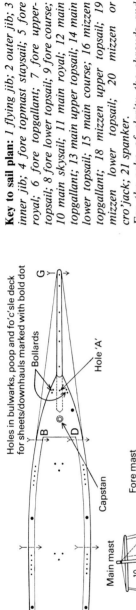

Holes in bulwarks, poop and fo'c'sle deck for sheets/downhauls marked with bold dot

Bollards

Hole 'A'

Capstan

Bollards

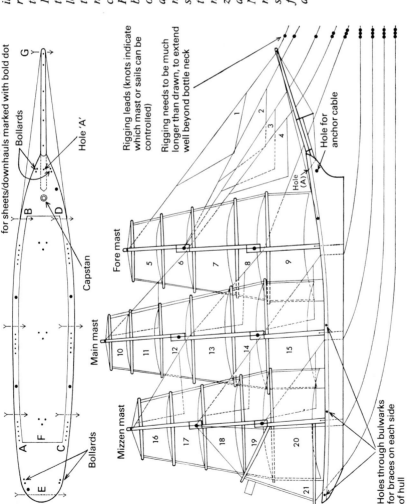

Rigging leads (knots indicate which mast or sails can be controlled)

Rigging needs to be much longer than drawn, to extend well beyond bottle neck

Fore mast

Main mast

Mizzen mast

Hole for anchor cable

Hole (A)

Holes through bulwarks for braces on each side of hull

Fig 14: *Sail plan of a clipper ship for a bottle.*

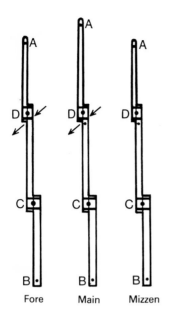

Fore   Main   Mizzen

Left, Fig 15: *Mast detail, showing the three sections and where the various holes have to be drilled. (Not to scale.)*

Below right, Fig 16: *Yards required for the clipper ship model described in this chapter (Not to scale.)*

Below far right, Fig 17: *Clove hitch on yards, and reef knot.*

finally glasspaper. Next cut out bulwarks making them no less than $^1/_{16}$ in wide and $^3/_{32}$ in deep. The best way is to mark the bulwarks with a hard pencil and cut along the lengths A-B-C-D (see deck plan, fig 14) with the craft knife and cut out the fo'c'sle and poop decks with the chisel. The excess wood is then carefully cut away with the chisel, giving the deck a slight camber. Smooth with glasspaper, noting the 'run' of the grain.

Now is a good time to paint the inside of the bulwarks white, using a small piece of card to keep the paint off the deck. Should any go on it can be carefully sanded off. The holes, where indicated, should be drilled right through the hull, taking care to drill the bulwark holes at an angle towards the middle of the hull because of the curved section. The decks can now be varnished. Next drill the hole for the bowsprit, following the line of the hull sheer and making the hole about $^1/_2$ in deep by $^3/_{32}$ in wide. The bowsprit has to be a firm fixture as much of the rigging, topmast and topgallant and jib stays come through when erecting the masts and the stays are finally glued at this point.

The bowsprit is made from $^1/_{16}$ in dowelling some 2 in long, tapering towards the tip and pointed at the end which fits into the hull. Six vertical holes are drilled in this, four for the jib and for the topmast stays, and one for the Dolphin Striker, which is made from a fine needle preferably painted white with the eye downwards to take the Dolphin Striker or martingale stays and bowsprit guys. To rig the bowsprit, affix the Dolphin Striker so that the top is flush with the upper surface of the bowsprit. Drill a hole right through the deck to come out at the position indicated 'a'. Thread the needle, knot the end of the cotton, and pass it down through hole 'a', loop it round the Dolphin Striker, then through the horizontal hole at the end of the bowsprit (G), through the hole B, across the deck, through hole D and knot securely at G, trimming off the end after glueing. Drill a hole in the position shown for the anchor cable just above hole 'a' at each side of the bows.

For the masts (see fig 15) you will need $^1/_{16}$ in dowelling cut to the required lengths (depending, of course, on the ship being modelled), each section tapering towards the topgallant mast and drilled at the truck (A) and the heel (B) (for the mast hinges), at the crosstree-mast doublings and in the case of the fore and main masts, where shown by the arrows in fig 15, the holes being drilled diagonally, and in the main and mizzen masts just below the topgallant mast doublings. The sections of masts are glued and clove hitched at the top and bottom of each doubling and look effective painted white at this part. Many clippers had their lower masts all white and the top mast and topgallant mast buff-coloured. White should be used sparingly on small models though, as it has the effect of making parts look bigger.

Finish the masts with a thin coat of clear varnish. Cut three lengths of wire $1\frac{1}{4}$ in long and bent into 'U' shapes to form hinges for the masts, the wire going right through the hull and any excess being filed off. Glue these wires before inserting but make sure that none touches the masts. Your masts are now stepped into the hull, and rigging can begin. Tie a knot in the end of a 24 in length of brown or black Sylko and thread the first (foremast) shroud upwards through the hull, through the mast doublings at C in fig 15 and back through the opposite hole in the bulwarks, repeating this through the next two bulwark holes working aft. Then the topmast stays are threaded through at point D down through the bulwarks and then back up through the topgallant mast truck at A. Cant the mast slightly back towards the stern and then knot the whole of the loops of rigging to tighten all shrouds and backstays. Repeat for all three masts, making sure that all rigging is taut and that all three masts slope uniformly. This is a quite a lengthy job, of course, though in print it sounds quick and casual!

The yards are made from toothpicks cut to dimensions which suit your model, tapered towards each end and round in section. (Fig 16 shows the yards required for this model.) A hole is drilled $\frac{1}{16}$ in from each end of each yard and the various stays are then rigged as shown earlier in fig 13, being securely fastened to the masts with a slip knot and glued. Remember to make these of a length sufficient to protrude from the bottle neck at least 8 in. Also it is a good plan to knot the ends of the stays. One knot for foremast, two for main and three for mizzen mast stays will indicate which stay operates which mast, as described for the earlier models.

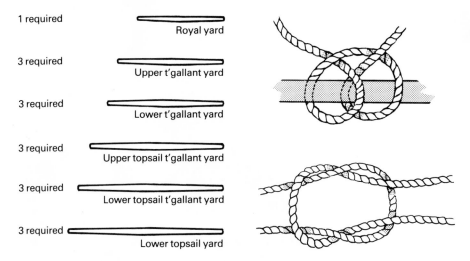

1 required — Royal yard

3 required — Upper t'gallant yard

3 required — Lower t'gallant yard

3 required — Upper topsail t'gallant yard

3 required — Lower topsail t'gallant yard

3 required — Lower topsail yard

Now is the time to screw the model to a base to keep the various mast stays taut whilst the yards are tied to their respective positions on the masts. Use the working base as described in the gadgets section of Chapter 1. The two nails driven into the end act as a cleat to wind the excess rigging around, which will eventually erect the masts and put the spanker sail in its proper position. Yards are clove hitched at their centres and tied to the masts with a reef knot which anyone should be able to tie. (Drawings of the reef knot and clove hitch are given in fig 17). Put a spot of adhesive on each knot, allow to dry and trim off close. Use buff cotton on top and topgallant masts and white if you paint the lower masts that colour.

The braces are now fitted to the yards, the main lower and upper topsail yards squared off and the threads tied at one end with an ordinary slip knot. Thread down through the bulwarks across the deck and up to the opposite end of the yards. Tie with an ordinary overhand knot which can be glued and trimmed off when dry. The braces for the lower, upper topgallant and royal yards are taken through the holes previously drilled in the masts (main and mizzen) $\frac{1}{8}$ in below the doublings at D in fig 15 and a hole drilled in the mizzen mast $\frac{1}{2}$ in below truck. The spanker sail can now be glued to the gaffs, the sail being curved by rolling it on your knee with a piece of $\frac{1}{8}$ in dowel or a similar round object.

Take a length of brown or black Sylko (whichever you have chosen for your brace colour) about 24 in long, and thread through the upper topsail crosstrees leaving an inch for securing later. Then take it through the upper and lower gaffs at the after ends, through the hull at hole E and back through hole F. Lead the end up through the lower and upper gaffs (forward ends) to the crosstrees, and knot with the inch of thread you left there, pulling the knot back into the hole in the crosstrees and glueing. Then pull the thread loop so that your sail is in position with a nice curve, and glue at the four gaff points.

The sails are now cut from your bond paper, curved in the same way as your spanker sail. Hold these up to the yards to check that they almost touch the yard below when in their curved shape and that the lower corners of fore course, main course and crossjack are level with the bulwarks. The sails are glued with a $\frac{1}{16}$ in band of glue to the front of, and flush with, the top of the yards. The staysails are glued to the stays. Use only sparingly or the glue will in time stain the sails. Care must be taken to place your main topgallant staysail near to the foremast to allow clearance when the masts and yards are folded flat. Failure to do this will prevent the masts lying down snugly. Now fit the flying, outer and inner jibs and fore topmast staysail. Incidentally, many clipper ships had a fore and aft sail called a main spencer (similar to that on the mizzen mast). This, of course, has been omitted on the grounds of impracticability on a bottle model.

A tip of white enamel at the end of each yard, the gaffs and mast trucks will improve your model, but make sure not to let any run on to the braces. A touch of white $\frac{1}{16}$ in above the bulwarks and $\frac{1}{16}$ in wide across the shrouds will also help the overall attractive look of the rigging. Then test your model for folding and swivelling the yards and take care to overlap each sail over the one below it, thus avoiding any crumpling. The capstan is made from a large pin painted grey or white and cut so that it stands $\frac{1}{16}$ in above the fo'c'sle deck.

Preparing the bottle

Remove all wire and labels, wash out the bottle thoroughly in hot water and leave upside down to dry. Roll your blue Plasticine into sections as round as your little finger and about 6 in long and insert the rolls vertically through the bottle neck. Spread the first one round one edge to a depth of about $\frac{1}{2}$ in, repeating at the other edge. Five of these should be sufficient to cover the bottom of the bottle, remembering that the middle of the bottle is raised and so the Plasticine should be pressed down until the surface is fairly level. Then, using the spoon-ended rod (see fig 3) waves can be formed in the surface. Spread a minute roll of white at the back of the bottle to give an effect of the ship's wake and apply tiny spots of white spread out thinly on the wave crests. Finally, make sure that the bottle neck is perfectly clean, ready to receive the model. If desired, a cardboard template the same shape as the hull base can be placed in the bottle to give an idea of the space it will occupy. Press this in and build the Plasticine up to the card. This will ensure that your model can be pressed into the sea in a prepared position to remain firm whilst the rigging is finally tightened. Remove the card template with a wire. Do *not* place any glue or adhesive of any kind on the base where your model will rest. If any rigging tangles whilst your model is in the process of being erected, it might stay that way! The Plasticine and excess rigging thread are sufficient to hold the model securely.

When folding the model for insertion into the bottle, first roll up the spanker sail like a cigarette and be careful to avoid crumpling any square sails when overlapping them. When the ship is part way in the bottle begin pulling on the stays, working with the mizzen, main and foremasts in that order. Any rigging which tangles can be eased using a piece of wire with its last $\frac{3}{8}$ in bent at a right angle. Care should be taken when pulling this wire out again so that it doesn't catch in anything else. The hull of the model should be firmly pressed down into the sea now and all rigging hauled taut, making sure that the yards are at right angles to the masts. At the five points on the bowsprit a small dab of adhesive should be placed just before the jib stays, and the foremast stays hauled taut.

All the rigging threads outside the bottle neck should now be fastened temporarily with an elastic band or a piece of Plasticine on the outside of the bottle while the glue sets. The jib stays are then cut off close under the bowsprit and the rest of the rigging stays which come from under the hull are cut off just inside the bottle neck and the excess 'buried' under the sea. A small bow wave at each side of the bows topped with white and also a very small white streak at intervals along both sides of the hull completes the effect.

Now for the deck fittings. Some modellers put these in first, but I never do as all the space you can spare on deck level is to the good and saves damage to sails, yards and masts when the model is pushed into the bottle. This should never be a tight fit or all your hours of work will be ruined. Most clipper ships had two or three deckhouses, three hatches, a wheelhouse (sometimes also a chartroom), curved companion ways and usually three boats, two on davits and one (keel side up) on top of one of the forward deck houses. Some had henhouses and pigsties, and don't forget the galley with its characteristic chimney. Access to the fo'c'sle deck and poop were by ladders on the port and starboard sides. All these items should be made and tested for fitting before your model is equipped with sails. In particular, remember to drill the davit holes (if required) so that they are clear of the crojack and main course sails.

Deck equipment

Deck houses can be made very simply from thin tin or aluminium, or even those metal plates used on small offset litho printing machines. Cut to shape as shown in fig 18 and score gently where the edges fold down, to form a box. The ports can be drilled with a No 70 drill, and the doors can be made of black or brown paper. The deck houses should be given a coat of glue inside to hold them squarely, and painted to suit. A small piece of wood is glued inside to fit to the underside of the roof of the deck house, making sure it is just slightly less than the height of the deck house. This piece of wood will 'anchor' the deck house securely to the deck. File the short ends slightly concave to fit the camber of the deck. NB, all deckhouses, hatches, companion ways, etc, were usually rounded off to avoid crew injury in rough seas.

The galley, with chimney made from a headless pin, painted black, can be made the same way, and so can hatches. The wheel house (see fig 18) usually had a sloping or curved roof and one of those small toothed wheels on the winder of a wrist-watch makes an ideal helm. Paint the wheel house white, with the roof the same shade as the deck houses and the wheel dark brown. **Ship's boats** can be made quite easily from a flattened out toothpaste tube (cleaned out first!). Cut as shown in fig 19, then open the folded tube slightly with a pin or tweezers and nip each end firmly. File slightly round at each end of the keel and put a thin line of glue where the bow and stern joints are. If you wish, small thwarts can be made from minute strips of bamboo and the inside of the boats can be painted buff and the outside white.

Davits can be made from bent headless pins (see fig 19), in which case incorporate two fine threads in the bow and stern joints of the boats and glue these to the other end of the davits. With a little patience (which you will have acquired by this stage!) these can be place in two holes at the inside of the bulwarks between your main and mizzen masts.

Flags (see fig 20) can be cut from illustrated magazines and glued to the spanker halyard. Some plastic ship kits include small printed paper flags which can be used sometimes. If you are handy with a soldering iron **anchors** (see fig 21) can be made from brass pins by flattening the head of the pin with a small hammer and drilling a hole through the flattened head. Flatten another pin for the stock and drill a hole in the centre. Make the flukes in a similar way and bend. Solder together the three parts and file afterwards. The stock should taper at each end and remember it should be at right angles to the flukes. Anchors were stowed on the fo'c'sle. **Bollards** for bow and stern can be made from small pins cut down to $1/8$ in, placed $1/16$ in apart. Be careful when drilling holes for these because your bows are concave at this part and also curved at the counter (astern).

Figureheads improve the look of a model and can be made quite easily from celluloid collar stiffeners shaped with a small file. There are some varied figureheads on board *Cutty Sark*, a really fine collection. The colouring of some of these is remarkable and will give a good idea of what will be suitable for your model.

The deck houses can be manipulated into position on the end of your thin wire with just a dab of adhesive on the underside. When you are completely satisfied that your model is perfectly dry and all yards squared to your liking, wipe the inside of the bottle neck with a damp piece of bandage or cotton wool (or wind it round your little finger) to eradicate any glue marks. Get a good tight fitting cork, glue the edge all round and press in flush, finishing off with sealing wax, filed smooth. If you like, put on a Turk's Head knot. This knot is started

Fig 18: *Making deck houses and wheel house. (Not to scale.)*

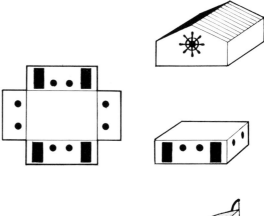

Fig 19: *Boats made from metal toothpaste tube, using headless pins for davits. (Not to scale.)*

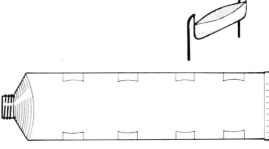

Fig 20: *Miniature flags can be cut and folded from illustrated colour magazines. (Not to scale.)*

Fig 21: *If you are skilled with a soldering iron, realistic anchors can be made from pins, as described in the text. (Not to scale.)*

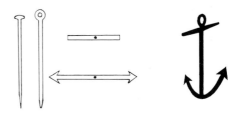

off very similarly to a clove hitch. Cross the two parts in the same direction as the original cross and pass one end through and follow the end round to produce two or three parts (this looks like plaiting we all made at school). Pull taut and tuck the ends under after cutting off short, glue and paint the whole lot, knot and cork, in any colour to suit; gold, red or white look most effective. If in doubt about the method of tying these knots, your library will find you a helpful book on this subject.

The *Cutty Sark*

This remarkable composite clipper ship of 966 tons, perhaps the most famous of all, was built in 1869 by Scott and Linton at Dumbarton for John Willis, a former sailing ship master who retired to become a London shipowner. So keen was the contract price for the vessel that the builders went bankrupt and she was eventually finished by William Denny & Bros. She was built for the express purpose of beating the passages set up by a clipper ship some writers class as her better, *Thermopylae*. The controversy over the various qualities of these rival ships has lasted more than a century and probably never will be settled. *Thermopylae* has gone and *Cutty Sark* remains.

Strange to say, these two ships only once raced each other and that was three years after *Cutty Sark* was completed. The outcome was still unsatisfactory as to the question of the two clippers' vaunted merits because, although *Cutty Sark* had established a formidable lead over her rival, she lost her rudder whilst in the Indian Ocean. A jury rudder was made and fitted in less than a week in gale force conditions, a remarkable feat of joinery and seamanship combined. So under this handicap she arrived in port a week after *Thermopylae* and consequently the great question was never answered as to which was the fastest ship. *Cutty Sark* often carried well over a million-and-a-quarter pounds of tea and often exceeded 300 miles a day.

She carried her last tea cargo eight years after her completion and from then on whatever cargoes were available, such as coal, wood, wool, palm sugar and even scrap iron. She was sold to the Portuguese in 1895 who sailed her for the next 27 years. They cut down her rig to a barquentine and renamed her *Ferreira*. Between 1920 and 1922 she was run by a Lisbon firm of shipowners, then in 1922 she returned to London. Luckily for posterity Fate stepped in for, whilst on her way back to Portugal, she was forced back to Falmouth by adverse weather and was seen by Captain Dowman, who had once watched her pass the ship he was then serving on as a young seaman. Being a man of some means he decided to make an offer for her and finally obtained possession for £3,750. So she returned to her native land and was restored by Captain Dowman in Falmouth, a job which lasted until 1924. She spent several years in that harbour and, on Captain Dowman's death, his widow presented her, together with a generous sum of money for maintenance, to the Thames Nautical Training College. She made her last sea voyage towed by a tug to join the training ship HMS *Worcester*. When *Worcester* (an old ship) was subsequently broken up, *Cutty Sark*'s future became uncertain, a steel-built ship having come into the possession of the College.

The old clipper was moored off Greenwich and became one of the sights of the Festival of Britain in 1951. Luckily, His Royal Highness the Duke of Edinburgh, interested in all nautical matters, formed what was later to become the Cutty Sark Preservation Society, with the object of raising £250,000 to restore the ship to her former glory. The Thames Nautical Training College presented the ship to the Society as a free gift and her registry certificate was handed over in 1953 to the patron of the Society, the Duke of Edinburgh.

The dry dock at Greenwich which she now occupies was most generously built on a non profit basis and the re-rigging was undertaken on the same terms. The ship finally completed restoration in 1957 and was opened to the public after a ceremony by Her Majesty the Queen and Prince Philip. Thus a great ship,

The Cutty Sark *has a permanent home at Greenwich and is well worth a visit. She makes a good subject for a bottle model, with just minor modifications to the rig.*

unquestionably one of the fastest and best-built of all time, is now permanently preserved for the nation as a fitting reminder of the great days when England was a power to be reckoned with in the world of sail.

The name *Cutty Sark*, which means a short shift or shirt, was taken from Robert Burns' poem *Tam O'Shanter*. When Tam, after a hard night's drinking passed the Church of Kirk Alloway riding his horse he was amazed to see a number of witches dancing, all extremely ugly except one, whose name was Nannie, wearing of course the aforementioned garment. When Tam applauded all went dark and poor Tam had to flee for his very life to the Doon Bridge, knowing that witches cannot cross water. Nannie, however, being fleeter of foot (and one would imagine younger), seized the horse's tail which came away in her hand. If you look at a photograph of the ship, or better still visit her at Greenwich, you will see the figurehead of Nannie with her left arm outstretched, reaching for the horse's tail.

Apart from the beautiful sight the ship presents from the outside there is aboard her now a most interesting collection of models, relics, booklets, plans and possibly the finest collection of figureheads to be seen anywhere. She is a must for anyone interested in sailing ships, so make a point of seeing her when you are in London.

In contrast to the way in which *Cutty Sark* has been preserved, her contemporary and closest rival *Thermopylae* was bought by the Portuguese Navy in 1896 and was renamed *Pedro Nunes*. The next year she was discarded, having served for a short time as a school-ship and was used as a coal hulk until 1907. In the autumn of that year she was sunk by two torpedoes fired by a Portuguese Navy torpedo boat during a naval review, a tragic end indeed for such a wonderful ship.

When one looks at the bows of the ship, almost knife-like, it is easy to picture her racing home at anything around 16 knots, carrying 32,000 sq ft of sail, on another record-breaking voyage. *Cutty Sark* makes a fine subject for a bottle model and I have seen many in my travels around the country. The average modeller can make an excellent model of the ship and if in doubt about any details, can, for the price of a train ticket, see and go aboard the actual ship in dry dock at Greenwich. Diagrams are given here with a simplified rigging plan to suit its inclusion in a bottle. The only difficulty is the fore and aft sail on the main lower mast, which was known as a 'spencer'—a lot of model makers prefer to ignore this but for an accurate model it really is essential to include this sail. Whether this particular sail was much use is a matter of debate, but I have certainly included it in all the bottle models I have made of this ship. The fact that these spencer sails disappeared from use after only a relatively few years in service and the traditional triangular staysails returned, points to the fact that perhaps they were not a roaring success.

The bottle I used for this model was a 1 pint Haig dimple but these are difficult to obtain nowadays, although there must be several hundreds left tucked away somewhere! The modern dimple bottles no longer have the name deeply etched on the side and, unfortunately, the neck aperture is smaller, but this can be easily got over by making the hull a little shallower.

As so many people ask the inevitable question 'How long does it take to make a ship on a bottle?' I did, in this case, add up the hours taken to build this model from scratch. It proved to be around 60 hours although a more complicated model can take much, much longer and so the modeller is wise if he only works

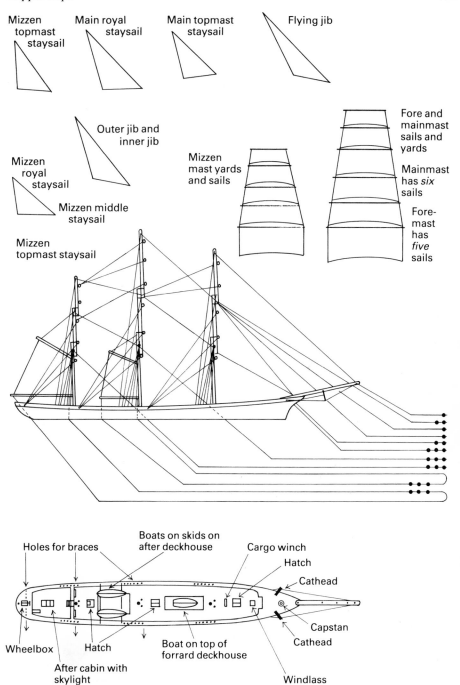

Fig 22: *Sail plan for the* Cutty Sark *and plan showing the positions of the holes for deck fittings and braces.*

for about 2 hours at any one time. With miniature models in particular this is quite enough, for if one attempts to do more the quality of the work will suffer. Personally I make a point of never working under artificial light as daylight is far and away the best, (despite what the various strip lighting firms might say!). The advice given in Chapter 6 (*'A clipper ship for a large dimple bottle'*) for the general carving and rigging instructions are pretty much the same for the *Cutty Sark,* except for the spencer sail and the fact that this ship had less curved sheer-lines. The hull colour of *Cutty Sark* is black with white lines painted parallel to the sheer and at the waterline. The hull below the waterline was Muntz metal which can be indicated by Humbrol copper paint, but, as the modeller may well have a bottle with a narrow neck, it will not be possible to include this. Always make the width of the hull half the diameter of the bottle neck, but preferably less, this will save any trouble later with the 'top-hamper', ie, masts, yards, sails, etc, not to mention the space taken up with the excess rigging threads which come under the hull.

There are a lot of romantic paintings in existence showing *Cutty Sark* under an enormous press of sail, with studding sails billowing out in seas which would scare the pants off any master in sail! Even famous painters have had criticism levelled at them by sailing-ship captains, for in such mountainous seas as are depicted the ship would be carrying only a minimum of sail. But the pictures *look* impressively romantic and certainly sell! In any case, the narrow confines of a dimple bottle do not easily permit the inclusion of studding sails so the average modeller would be best advised to forget these. The *Cutty Sark* in the course of her career, had many different colour schemes but at present her lower masts, spencer-gaff, spanker boom and gaff and the bowsprit, as far as the Dolphin Striker, are white with yards, topmast and topgallant masts in black, (although I have seen these latter painted a very dark brown). The best guide is to send for an illustrated colour postcard from the ship-retail shop on board for many models I have seen have been utterly spoiled by the attachment of a great number of flags and most of *them* flying in the wrong direction! Normally the ship would have had the red ensign flying at the peak of the spanker gaff and the house flag at the mainmast head. The house flag of John Willis & Son consists of a red cross on a white diamond on a dark blue background.

I have a particularly fine three-dimensional colour picture card of this ship which I purchased from a gift shop at Boppard on the Rhine some 15 years ago and I have never seen another. Although only a postcard it looks as though it is about ½ in thick, but again the ship is shown carrying every stitch of sail in what looks like a Force 7 gale. Had the ship been carrying that amount of sail she would not now be at Greenwich!

The hull for this model is made from a length of hardwood 4¾ in long × $^{11}/_{16}$ in square and carved out in the same way as described for the clipper ship model (see Chapter 6) but note from the plan that *Cutty Sark* is slightly different at bow and stern. After carving out the well deck, drill the holes for the shrouds and backstays, sanding the width down afterwards. Test the hull width in case the bottle you have has a very narrow neck, remembering that some tolerance must be allowed for paint and braces on each side of the hull. All other instructions for clipper ship models apply to this one, save for the spencer sail, which only has a gaff at the head of the sail, but this is rigged as for the fore and aft sail on the mizzen and rolled up in the same manner for insertion in the bottle. The spencer sail has to be rolled up particularly tightly or it will crease.

Two of the author's models of the Cutty Sark; *one in a large and the other in a small dimple bottle (David Muscroft).*

The after cabin has five port holes at each side and the sides are painted white, as are the roofs of the two deckhouses and the boats. The roof of the after cabin is painted brown (or stained) as are the sides of the deckhouses. The two hatches are painted black on top with white sides. The wheelhouse is painted brown and the capstan white. I made the anchors on this model from tiny brass pins as described earlier in this chapter. The lower masts are painted in white, together with the mast doublings, mast heads and the ends of the yards. The skylight on the after cabin was indicated by a tiny square of a silver coloured foil paper. The model when completed was corked with the original plastic cap, painted red and embellished with a Turk's Head knot.

This model was amongst those exhibited at the First North American Exposition of Ships-in-Bottles at San Diego in 1982 on board the restored sailing ship *Star of India* and after many thousands of miles by parcel post arrived back unscathed.

Chapter 7

Sailing ships of the post-clipper era

After the wood, composite and iron hulled clippers had outlived their usefulness, much bigger ships, longer and loftier, were brought into being and one shipping company alone had 12 iron ships, all four-masted square-riggers, built in as many years, and all averaging 2,000 tons. From the latter end of the 19th century until 1905, when the last big square-rigger, the famous barque *Archibald Russell* (2,385 tons), was built on the Clyde, the Scottish yards turned out some remarkable iron and steel cargo carrying vessels. The *Archibald Russell* survived until after the Second World War, during which period she served as a floating grain 'warehouse' and was not finally broken up until 1949 at Gateshead. Originally this barque had painted ports (said by some to be a survival from the days of the East Indiamen which had dummy gun ports to deter piracy in the far eastern waters) but later she was painted black. This greatly detracted from her appearance, but still could not hide her beautiful lines.

Most of the biggest sailing ships were built after 1900 with one exception, *Potosi*. The *Potosi*, built in 1895, was a five-masted barque, ie, square-rigged on all masts except the last which was fore and aft rigged. She was owned by Laeisz of the famous Flying 'P' Line and registered in Hamburg. The French also had a magnificent fleet of sailing ships and the *France II* of Bordeaux was the biggest sailing vessel ever built, 5,633 tons. This barque was fitted with an auxiliary engine. These huge ships had steel masts, yards and wire and chain rigging and several rounded Cape Horn under full sail, they were so well founded and strongly constructed.

Ships of this period were principally engaged in the nitrate or guano trades, going from France, Germany, England and Scandinavian countries right round Cape Horn up to ports on the west coast of South America where such stuff was found in quantity. Guano was not a popular cargo because of its offensive smell and other undesirable qualities, but it was a very great source of revenue. These guano deposits, which had accumulated for hundreds of years, were seabird droppings and their properties as fertilizers were known hundreds of years before white man set foot in South America.

The ports of call were mere shanty towns and relied on the sale of this product for their very existence; who hears of the ports of Iquique, Tocopilla and Coquimbo now? Yet, in those far off days, they were the Mecca of the nitrate ships and the Germans had the loading and unloading of their ships (known to seafarers as 'turn round') down to a fine art. The more passages a 5,000-ton ship could make the greater the profits for the owners, to whom money was a major concern. These owners, though, kept their ships in fine condition although the cargo they engaged in was one which had a very adverse effect on canvas sails and also the sacks in which the guano was itself stowed. So the resultant unloading was unpleasant, unpopular with the crews, and distinctly odiferous and messy. But until the discovery of chemical fertilizers this was a distinctly profitable cargo which made fortunes for shipowners right up to 1939.

Wheat from Australian ports was another cargo much sought after and some remarkable passages were made by these huge cargo ships which often carried over 40,000 bags of wheat, at speeds which would not have disgraced the earlier and lighter clippers. One owner of probably the last and largest fleet of grain ships was Gustaf Erikson of Mariehamn, Finland. He has been criticised by some writers as being mean and parsimonious, but he was in reality a shrewd businessman and opportunist. During the years following the First World War he bought ships at near scrap prices, refitted them and sent them back to sea.

With such small crews the sailors jolly well *had* to be seamen to survive and though they often grumbled at their owners' shortcomings they were, with few exceptions, loyal and remarkable men. Ruben de Cloux was such a man. Of great stature and tremendous ability, he knew how to get the best out of his ship and crew. One of his commands was Erikson's famous ship, *Herzogin Cecilie*, built as a German cadet ship in 1902 and still a beautiful and well-founded ship right up until the time she met a tragic end, running aground on the Hamstone Rock at Salcombe in 1936 in thick fog, after winning the grain race following a passage of 86 days from Boston Island to Falmouth. I shall return to this ship, as she was a truly remarkable vessel in many ways.

Incidentally, Gustaf Erikson was also the owner of the *Archibald Russell* in the mid-1930s. There was a large collection of these big ships off Boston Island early in 1936, when *Herzogin Cecilie, Viking, Olivebank, Winterhude, Archibald Russell, L'Avenir, Penang* and *Pommern* prepared to make the long journey back to Europe with Australian grain. Some idea of the size of these ships can be imagined when it is realised that the fore, main and mizzen course yards were, in the case of the five-masted barques, over 100 ft long and weighed between eight and nine tons. The sails these yards carried were hand sewn from 24 in wide bolts of Arbroath canvas and would average a ton in weight—and that was when dry! The mainmast of the *Preussen* measured, from heel to truck, 223 ft, and the total length of her standing and running wire rigging together was 88,818 ft. Then the hemp rigging measured a total of 56,613 ft. She carried 47 sails, with a total area of something in the region of 50,000 sq ft. When this is compared with *Cutty Sark*'s sail area of 32,000 sq ft one can imagine what a gigantic and wonderful ship *Preussen* was; her tonnage was 5,080 tons gross.

As with most things like steam locomotives, electric trams and perhaps bicycles, by the time they reached ultimate perfection their years were numbered. *Preussen* was built in 1902 and was wrecked off Dover eight years later, having consistently averaged 11 knots for many voyages to South America and back to Germany. She was truly one of the most remarkable ships of all time. *Potosi*, a very similar vessel in some respects to *Preussen* but barque rigged, was built by the same concern, J.C. Tecklenborg of Geestemunde, and had a gross tonnage of 4,026. *Potosi*, which once made a voyage from Tocopilla to the English Channel in the record time of 56 days, was in South America throughout the whole of the First World War, and like many other sailing vessels was handed over to France as war reparations and was not recommissioned until five years after the cessation of hostilities. She was then owned in Valparaiso and renamed *Flora*. This ship was unfortunately lost by fire in 1925.

The last five-masted barque was built in 1921, the Danish schoolship *Köbenhavn*, and was probably the finest sail training ship ever to sail the seas. Like *Potosi* she had a divided spanker sail when she was first built—an uncommon rig except in German shipbuilding yards—and this was later replaced by a single spanker. *Köbenhavn*, which was from the yard of Messrs Ramage and Ferguson, of Leith, sailed from Buenos Aires to proceed to Adelaide and was never seen again. It is generally assumed that she hit an iceberg in fog sometime between December 1928 and January 1929 and this huge vessel of 3,901 tons sank, taking with her a crew of 59 which included cadets. The only trace ever found was a lifebelt bearing the letters *havn*, the rest having been obliterated.

In 1939 Gustaf Erikson was the last of the big sailing ship owners and had ten three- or four-masted barques in commission. They were *Pamir* (which sank in a hurricane in 1957), *Passat, Pommern* (now a floating museum in Mariehamn), *Archibald Russell, Viking* (now at Gothenburg), *Winterhude, Lawhill* (now hulked at Laurenco Marques), *Killoran, Moshulu* (which made the fastest grain race passage home that year of 91 days), and *Olivebank*, which struck a German mine near Esbjerg on her way back to the Baltic on September 12, 1939, nine days after the outbreak of the Second World War, taking down with her the captain and 13 of the crew. The last of the Flying 'P' Line of sailing ships to be built and owned by Franz Laiesz, *Padua* (built in 1926), also took part in the last grain race and was just two days behind the winner.

The other ships participating in this memorable and historic event were *Abraham Rydberg* (Abraham Rydberg Association) and *Kommodore Johnsen* (Norddeutscher Lloyd). When one considers the wages seamen were paid, even at that date, one realises that men must surely have been dedicated to follow the sea. Remuneration certainly wasn't the attraction, for an ordinary seaman's pay for a *month* was £2, an apprentice's 10/-, and an able seaman's £2 10s! The sailmaker (who in the course of a voyage would have to maintain three suits of sails) could expect £6 and the captain £20. So a cargo-carrying era by sailing ships of this tonnage came to a close with the outbreak of the Second World War. The world will never see their like again and is the poorer for their passing.

The *Preussen*—the world's largest sailing ship

For more years than I care to remember there have been discussions in countless magazines concerning the sea and sailing ships, as to which sailing ship was the largest. In terms of displacement tonnage the *France II* was the largest sailing *vessel*, albeit an auxiliary sailing ship, but the pure definition of a ship is 'a vessel of three of more masts, square-rigged on all masts'. So although the *France II* displaced some 5,663 tons (some versions vary) and was 418 ft long she was a five-masted *barque*, ie, the aftermost mast was fore and aft rigged. So, the *Preussen* (5,080 tons) being the *only* five-masted square-rigged ship is the only contender for this much discussed title. Had it been possible to stand this ship alongside Nelson's column, her mainmast of 223 ft, from keel to truck, she would have towered 53 ft above Horatio's head! Owned by Ferdinand Laeisz of the famous Flying 'P' Line, she was registered in Hamburg.

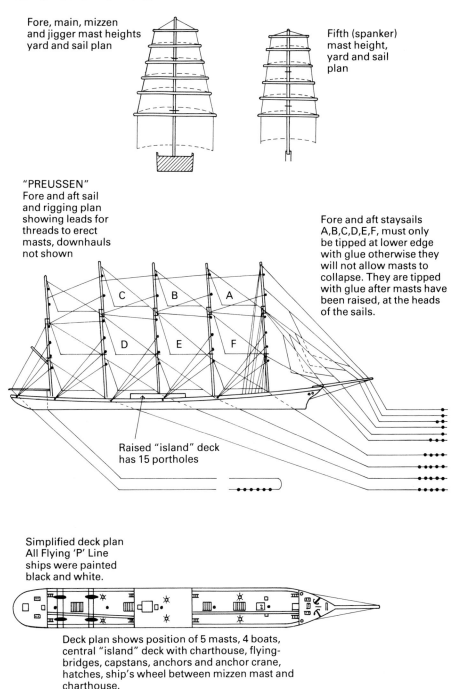

Fore, main, mizzen and jigger mast heights yard and sail plan

Fifth (spanker) mast height, yard and sail plan

"PREUSSEN"
Fore and aft sail and rigging plan showing leads for threads to erect masts, downhauls not shown

Fore and aft staysails A,B,C,D,E,F, must only be tipped at lower edge with glue otherwise they will not allow masts to collapse. They are tipped with glue after masts have been raised, at the heads of the sails.

C   B   A
D   E   F

Raised "island" deck has 15 portholes

Simplified deck plan All Flying 'P' Line ships were painted black and white.

Deck plan shows position of 5 masts, 4 boats, central "island" deck with charthouse, flying-bridges, capstans, anchors and anchor crane, hatches, ship's wheel between mizzen mast and charthouse.

Fig 23: *Sail and deck plan for a model of the* Preussen.

Like many ships of this era, the *Preussen* had lower and topmast in one single length. It has been said that this ship and her sister ship, *Potosi*, (which was a five-masted barque) were never passed at sea by any other ship, whether sail or steam and knowing of her impressive record I am inclined to believe this. From a model-makers viewpoint I would class this as one of the most difficult ships to put into a bottle, taking into consideration that there are 5 masts, 30 yards, 2 gaffs and 47 sails to get through a bottle neck, not to mention the hull and quite a lot of the deck fittings aft have to be *in situ* before insertion including four of the ship's boats. Thus, the modeller will understand the difficulties. However, with some patience, dedication, a long bottle with a reasonably wide bottle neck (and a comprehensive vocabulary) it *can* be done! In modern parlance, it is 'no pushover' but the end result more than compensates for the initial endeavour. I used a Bell's 1 pint whisky bottle which had a neck diameter of $^{11}/_{16}$ in but a slightly wider bottle neck would be an asset.

The hull of *Preussen* was 407 ft long and the beam $53^{1}/_{2}$ ft, so a long bottle is essential. The methods of rigging and building are similar to the square rigged ships described in other pages of the book and a plan of the ship suitable for a bottle model is illustrated in fig 23 (see previous page). A photo of the completed model is shown on page 86. To make things somewhat easier the height of the hull may be slightly reduced without detracting from the appearance of the model, as the *Preussen* often carried huge cargoes and consequently was much lower in the water. The hull for this model is $5^{1}/_{16}$ in $\times$ $^{5}/_{8}$ in and with the bowsprit is $5^{7}/_{8}$ in long overall. The fore, main, mizzen and jigger masts are all the same height, $2^{3}/_{16}$ in, and the fifth (spanker) mast is 2 in high. As can be seen *Preussen* crossed six yards on each mast and four of her five lower yards were 102 ft long and the royal yards $52^{1}/_{2}$ ft. Naturally the vast amount of rigging this ship carried (26 miles of it!) has had to be simplified for a bottle model but it has been kept as near as possible to the original. The vast amount of deck detail has, of necessity, been omitted on this small scale for a model of this size would look unbelievably cluttered up were it ever possible to reproduce every detail. This can be appreciated when it is realised that the ship had 10 sets of bollards, 22 brace winches, 6 main deck capstans, 8 accommodation ladders, apart from numerous skylights and ventilators. Thus, many of the minor deck fittings have been omitted from the plan. The number of shrouds and backstays have been reduced in quantity as well since it is not possible to drill the necessary holes so close together without them running into each other.

A famous miniature ship modeller, C. Hampshire, who is no longer with us once said, 'Obtain a photograph of the model you are going to make and what you *can't see*, leave out!' This gentleman once exhibited a model of the *Queen Mary* the same length as his fountain pen and although the ship had every porthole, many other details were, of course, omitted. I have seen many otherwise excellent models absolutely ruined by dozens of sheave blocks which, to the scale shown, would have been the same diameter as the capstan! If you incorporate *one* small item, you have to incorporate them *all*.

The *Preussen* had four ship's boats astern and as it would have been impossible to place these in afterwards they were put *in-situ*, but the majority of the fittings were placed in after the hull. For all the masts, yards, gaffs and sails, a ship of this complexity *has* to be a squeeze in a normal bottle. Notice that the downhauls for the fore, main, mizzen and jigger masts have been omitted from

This superb scale model of the Preussen *resides in San Francisco Maritime Museum, and gives bottle modellers a good idea of how she looked.*

the plan as these would only cause confusion. The braces for the spanker masts were also omitted.

The mizzen mast (the middle one) is hinged into the top of the central raised deck, which also adds to the bulk of the model in its folded state. But, with accuracy and patience *Preussen* can be safely bottled and I know personally six other modellers who have made extremely good models of her.

The *Preussen* had two raised flying bridges with the forrard one in line with the fore and aft centre of the ship and the after one angled. Should the modeller doubt his ability to include 47 sails, these can be omitted, as in the ship shown which is a 'bare pole' model. There are many such models in museums which actually look quite well and the rigging is, of course, more noticeable. In the latter days of sail, such as in all-steel ships like *Preussen*, the various yards were of the same length and interchangeable whereas in the days of the clipper ships the fore, main and mizzen yards were all of different lengths. Later on many four-masted steel ships were built only crossing five yards and thus were known as 'bald-headers'. One such ship was called *Pommern* which belonged to the Flying 'P' Line. Apparently this cut down rig did not affect speed too much, so quite a few were built.

The owners of some of the latter day ships were inclined to be a trifle parsimonious, so that there were less sails to replace in the event of damage at sea. Damage to sails occured quite often when the ships captain was a little remiss at taking in sail. Most sailing ships carried three 'suits' of sails, the oldest being kept for the warmer, calmer seas but a captain who, through negligence, ruined a good set of sails would be apt to lose his job unless he had a very good excuse.

In the 1930s cargo-carrying sailing ships were run on an absolute 'shoe string' and often only the cargo, not the ship, was insured. This, however, was long after *Preussen* had passed on for, she met her end in 1910 when she collided with

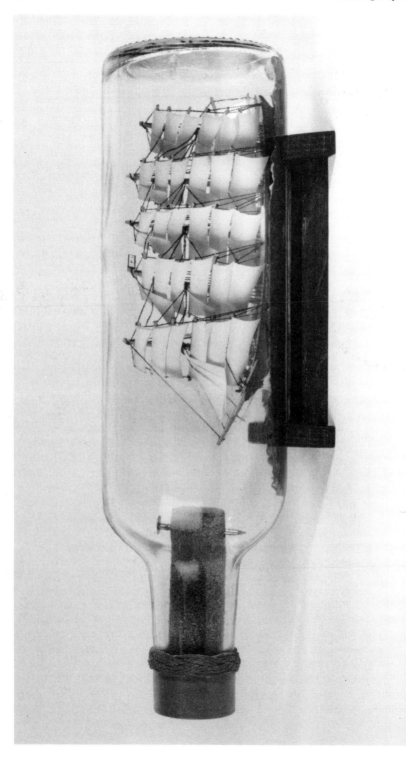

The five-masted ship Preussen, *made by the author. Note the pierced cork (described in Chapter 11).*

the cross-Channel steamer, *Brighton*, whose captain had under-estimated her speed. This happened between Dover and St Margaret's Bay. The captain of the cross-Channel steamer was held responsible for the collision but her end was particularly tragic for there, within sight of land, the greatest sailing ship in the world met her end. Twelve tugs tried in vain to get her afloat again, but without success, and traces of this magnificent ship can still be seen today at Fan Bay, some 70 odd years after her wreck.

The lower yards of *Preussen* weighed in the region of 10 tons, so it is easy to appreciate what an awe-inspiring sight she must have been at sea. Much has been said in recent years of building a new line of cargo-carrying sailing ships with some proposals envisaging ships of 12,000 tons, and simplified methods of rigging and labour-saving devices to cut down on the number of crew needed. There would seem to be no logical reason for not building a new fleet of ships such as these and at least there would be no danger of the present levels of oil pollution which decimate marine and sea life in our 'progressive' era. The main reason for the original demise of the big cargo-carrying sailing ships was the unpredictable delivery date for cargoes but with the use of auxiliary engines this problem could well be overcome.

Herzogin Cecilie

This German cadet ship, originally of 3,242 tons, was built by Rickmers of Bremerhaven in 1902 and carried a crew of 100 men and boys. She was one of the most famous ships ever known and was without a shadow of a doubt the second fastest sailing ship, having reached an authenticated speed of $20^3/4$ knots in 1931 in the Skaw, Northern Denmark, and in 1930 covered 365 miles in $23^1/2$ hours off the Cape of Good Hope.

Gustaf Erikson bought *Herzogin Cecilie* after the Germans had handed her over to the French as part of 1914-18 war reparations. Ships similar to *Herzogin Cecilie* in size and tonnage were purchased at that time for sums between £2,000-£3,000. Erikson saw her great potential as a contender in the grain trade in which she was greatly distinguished. After the captain, Ruben de Cloux, left *Herzogin* to go into partnership with another world-famous sailor, Commander Alan Villiers, when they purchased *Parma*, a former Flying 'P' ship, a younger man was promoted from first mate to captain; his name was Sven Eriksson and a kind of rapport was established between this man and his famous ship.

Also an Alander by birth, but no relation to the owner, this captain quickly became renowned for his sheer seamanship and humane but firm treatment of his crew, which often numbered as few as 18 men. He knew how to get the best out of his crew and the ship made some really fast passages home with grain. She had her share of misfortunes, too; once her donkey boiler, which provided steam power for various winches and capstans, blew up in Belfast with disastrous results and this entailed a costly bill for repairs. But this ship, which was so strongly constructed with typical Teutonic efficiency, survived many vicissitudes and in the 1930s, under her new captain, who was less than 30 years old, she often showed newer sailing ships the way home.

Sven Eriksson met and married Pamela Bourne (who, incidentally worked as a crew member on *Herzogin Cecilie* on a voyage home from Australia which lasted three months). She was the daughter of Sir Ronald Bourne, who was at one time South Africa's Secretary for Defence. Pamela Bourne was a most intelligent girl, had been presented at Court and had already gained fame as a

The author built this fine model of the Herzogin Cecilie. *Originally intended as a sailing model he later decided to display it in a perspex case. It has a hollow hull, made up of 13 laminations and the helms operate the rudder. The mechanisms are made of wrist-watch parts with some of the small cogs housed in the wheelbox at the stern. The model took just over two years to build and measures 28 × 15 × 5 in. A little too big for a bottle, but a useful reference photograph for those planning to make a bottle model.*

world traveller and authoress. Her book about *Herzogin Cecilie* is, in my humble estimation, one of the finest sea books ever published, telling as it does the story of this and many other grain and nitrate ships.

She shows in her book, *The Duchess,* a remarkable sense of humour, one might even say puckish. Yet, in parts, the story has an infinite quality of poignancy and even sadness as this recently married couple helplessly watched their beloved ship breaking up off the coast of South Devon after a triumphal record passage from Australia to England with over 52,500 bags of wheat in her hold. But for this mishap, for which no satisfactory explanation has ever been given, the ship would have been good enough for another quarter of a century of service and had the Government at that time only a shred of foresight she could have been refloated, repaired and reverted to a school ship for would-be young British seamen.

Of course, countries can always find money for war purposes, but a sound proposition such as *Herzogin Cecilie* presented during the first few weeks of her stranding just didn't interest officialdom.

Between the years 1955 and 1958 I built a large model of the ship, 28 in long, a pleasurable task which took over two years and just about as long in research before that. This ship model, which stands in a perspex case, has a laminated hull 1/8 in thick which is made up of 13 parts. The twin helms astern operate the rudder by means of watch parts, the two ship's bells are made from the brass ends of old ball pens and the poop rail is of packing case wire soldered on to 52 upright stanchions. The yards and masts are wood and the handrail supports on the yards were made from more than 636 pins, drilled and riveted into the yards and with the rails soldered on to the pins which had the tops removed. Eighty-six rigging screws made of steel were drilled by hand and the hull has no fewer than 72 miniature portholes.

The more time I spent in research, the greater my interest grew, and having been a lifelong cyclist I decided to make the journey from Sheffield to Salcombe in South Devon in 1959 to stand on the cliffs at Bolt Head and visit Starehole Bay where the unfortunate ship met her final ignominious and tragic end. Fate had deemed that it was to be a beautiful calm day and out there in the still waters I could just make out the lines of her steel hull. She has since been blown up as at low tide she was considered a menace to shipping. The fittings, such as the chartroom, captain's cabin, yards and sails, figurehead, etc, were taken back to Finland and are now in her home port, Mariehamn, in the Maritime Museum.

Herzogin Cecilie was built with a long high poop deck and a short well deck so that the crew could work in relatively dry conditions. A small bridge connected the poop deck with the fo'c'sle to avoid crossing the well deck in bad weather. Above the well deck were four ship's boats, two more being carried astern on cradles and hoisted out on davits. This ship is a difficult subject for a bottle model, but with some patience and dedication it can be done. There is a bottle model of the ship in the Maritime Institute of Ireland at St Michael's Wharf, Dun Laoghaire, which I presented to the Museum in September, 1963.

Sven Eriksson died of cancer in Cape Town in 1954 and Pamela Eriksson returned to his birthplace, Pellas, in the Aland Islands, Finland, where I believe she still resides.

Other books which tell of this beautiful ship are *Falmouth for Orders* by Alan Villiers, *The Tall Ships Pass* by W. L. A. Derby and *Mother Sea* by Elis Karlson, who was first mate and is an author of considerable talent. He now lives in well-deserved retirement in Salisbury, Zimbabwe. The people of the Aland Islands have for generations followed a seafaring life and Mariehamn between the 1920s and the mid 1930s was one harbour in the world where around a dozen big sailing barques could often be seen.

When Gustaf Erikson died his family still kept a few sailing ships but gradually went into steam. The last grain race, which incidentally is the title of an excellent book by Eric Newby, took place in 1939. It was won by *Moshulu* as I have already mentioned.

Chapter 8

Multi-masted schooners in America

At the turn of the century there were many five- and six-masted schooners in North America but sadly, to the best of my knowledge, there are now none left at all. These 'lumber' schooners, most of which were built on the Maine coast around Massachusetts, Connecticut and other locations in the 'Down Easters' country, used to carry sawn timber (lumber) as well as coal, granite and cement. Many owners, out to make a 'quick buck' overloaded these schooners to such an extent they were often pictured carrying deck cargo piled so high that the helmsman aft could scarcely see the bowsprit of the ship. These were the work-horses (the crews called them 'workhouses' or 'floating coffins', to give the more printable names!) of the coast and many sailed with only a few inches 'freeboard'—the bulwarks almost being down to the level of the sea. Many five- and six-masted schooners were sailed by crews of ten or eleven men and it was rumoured that some owners were not above painting a false Plimsoll Line above the original for, they reasoned, a ship built of and packed with wood could not sink! Naturally there was great reluctance on the part of the seamen to serve on these ships so only sheer desperation or a brush with the law would drive a man to sea in these ships. With the depression after the First World War, many of these schooners were laid up and left to rot although some were later put to use in the Prohibition days for moon-lighting and consequently sunk by the Revenue men. Others were moored alongside jetties and turned into floating gin-palaces or gambling casinos, where they rotted or were destroyed by fire. The only seven-masted schooner, *Thomas W. Lawson,* was one of the rare metal hulled ships.

Actually a five- or six-masted schooner is not a hard model to put in a bottle, in fact it is far easier than a square rigged ship. A long bottle is essential for this model to allow not only for the length of the hull but for the masts in their folded position which project well past the stern of the ship until erected. Most of these schooners carried a boat on davits at the extreme stern end of the hull which further complicates model construction, but this can be added after the masts have been fully erected. Providing the hull is not a tight fit in the bottle neck the main sails will 'wrap' round the underneath of the hull on the model's passage through the neck. With a little care these ships can be inserted with no danger of a creased sail, the gaff-topsails being fastened to the mast. Whilst a long schooner might not look as attractive as a square rigged ship these are quite interesting models to construct. Whilst a lot of modellers prefer to build a clipper or similar ship I prefer to try and portray as many different rigs as possible, for Exhibition experience has shown me how many people are unaware that ships like the five-, six- and seven-masted schooners ever existed.

A model of a typical six-masted schooner

This model is a six-masted schooner, of the 'Great Lakes' type, which were built in the early 1900s in the USA. The model hull was carved from hardwood $6\frac{1}{8}$ in × $\frac{7}{8}$ in with the bulwarks originally left $\frac{1}{8}$ in wide whilst the deck was carved out to a depth of $\frac{1}{16}$ in. The holes were drilled in the bulwarks which were then sanded down to $\frac{3}{32}$ in and it is advisable to do it this way so as to avoid splitting the bulwarks. Masts and bowsprit were made of $\frac{1}{16}$ in dowel. The bowsprit fits into a $\frac{1}{16}$ in hole in the bows which must be drilled to a depth of $\frac{1}{2}$ in to take the strain of hauling up six masts. The method of making this six-masted schooner was very much the same as described for the four-masted one in Chapter 4, but if desired an extra thread can be added to allow the modeller to control each mast individually. To do this fasten threads to the top of the sixth, fifth, fourth, third and second mast. Drill an extra hole in the deck forrard of the mast hinges and the thread from each of the masts is taken through the mast doublings of the mast immediately forrard of the one concerned, passing the thread through the *same hole* as the one above the mast doublings which is the continuous thread and is fastened at the extreme stern of the ship. The thread is then taken down immediately in front of the next mast forrard. This gives individual control to every mast and although it entails extra work it is very worthwhile.

The hull can be painted black, grey or dark red with a white line parallel to the sheer. This is neatly done with the sheerline groove and cotton method described in Chapter 1. The sails were made from good quality Bond paper and the gaff topsails attached to the after part of the masts with a dab of adhesive. Providing that there is a $\frac{1}{16}$ in clearance between the sides of the hull and the bottle neck it will be found that the long sails can be quite easily curved under the hull, complete with booms. (It is very important that the sails be securely attached to

A typical six-masted schooner of the 'Great Lakes' type.

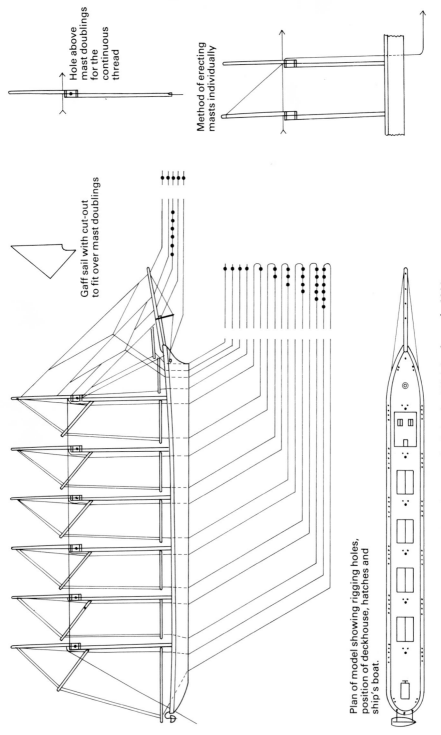

Hole above
mast doublings
for the
continuous
thread

Method of erecting
masts individually

Gaff sail with cut-out
to fit over mast doublings

Plan of model showing rigging holes,
position of deckhouse, hatches and
ship's boat.

Fig 24: *Plans for a six-masted schooner, such as was built in the USA in the early 1900s.*

both booms and gaffs.) One may see from the plan that the model has three shrouds and one backstay to each mast and, on the port side, an extra hole which is for the downhaul at the after end of each boom. The forrard downhaul is, of course, taken through the hole at the back of the mast hinge holes. The ship's boat was made of sheet tin and soldered directly on to the davits, which were made from brass pins. This method meant it was not too difficult to put the boat and davits in position into two holes drilled in the stern bulwarks. (Be careful not to drill these holes deeper than $1/16$ in or else the drill will come through the counter of the hull.) Masts, gaffs, booms and bowsprit should be painted a stone/buff colour, the deck can be 'bleached teak' and the ship's boat and deckhouse white. Hatches can be black or green on top with white sides while the two skylights on the forrard deckhouse can be indicated with two tiny sheets of silver paper. A long clear wine bottle is ideal for this model and mounted on a polished wooden stand it looks quite attractive.

Chapter 9

Ships in large bottles

In the course of the last two years I have made two ship models in Bell's 1 gallon whisky bottles. These bottles are $19^1/_2$ in long with a $5^1/_2$ in diameter. The ones I chose were of clear glass and free from the flaws which are often present in some large bottles. On one side of the bottle were three embossed words in the glass so this half of the bottle was painted over in pale blue (Humbrol No 47). This obliterated the lettering, provided a pleasing 'sky' background and showed up the white sails and rigging quite effectively.

One model I made is of a typical four-masted barque, with a hull of $7^3/_4$ in long and an overall length of 9 in. Surprisingly, for a bottle this size the neck aperture is only $1^1/_8$ in wide, so the hardwood hull was 1 in wide by $5/_8$ in thick. One of the advantages of a bottle model of this size is that the masts, yards and bowsprit are much more in proportion than in a ship model with a hull about 5 in long overall, in which the masts, yards and bowsprit *have* to be over scale to support the many holes which have to be drilled through them. So, with a large model like this one, all fittings can be much truer to scale. Not only that, but far more detail can be added, such as the accommodation ladders from the forecastle and poop decks, small portholes (made from brass pins), various bollards, ship's boats fitted with three thwarts etc. Mast caps can be added at the doublings, (which I made from thin sheet aluminium) so all the shrouds on the masts are absolutely correct, which is just not feasible on a small scale.

The four-masted barque model is virtually a scaled-down and adapted model of the *Preussen* in Chapter 8 and the proportions are such that the ship resting on its 'sea' of Plasticine has the fore, main and mizzen masts actually touching the top of the bottle.

The other model I made is a four-masted barquentine, which is square rigged on the fore mast and fore and aft rigged on the main, mizzen and jigger masts. This model has a tiny bottled miniature ship in the bottle neck as well! Working on a model in a bottle this length has its problems, so remember to leave the excess rigging threads correspondingly longer and have a good stock of fairly stout wires about 24 in long for jobs such as teasing out any 'snags' in rigging and wiping off glue smears. A $1/_4$ in diameter steel rod is also essential to place in the sea and mould the Plasticine into realistic waves. Keep a long wire at hand with a right angle bend in the last $1/_2$ in for placing in deck fittings. A stand of $5/_8$

Right, Fig 25: *Sails, simplified rigging and deck plan for a four-masted barque. (Shrouds and backstays are shown on the starboard side only.)*

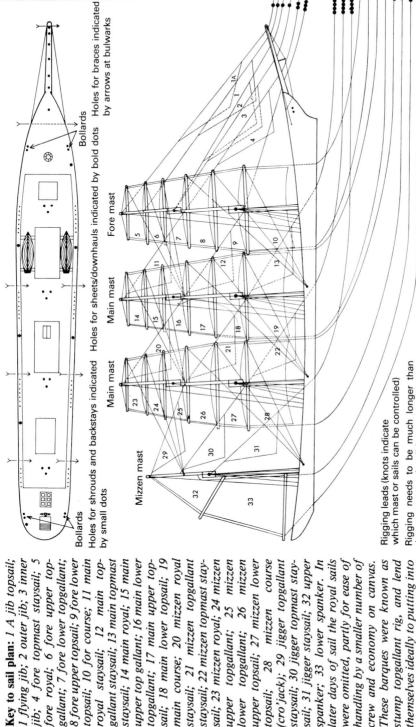

Bollards

Holes for braces indicated by arrows at bulwarks

Holes for sheets/downhauls indicated by bold dots

Fore mast

Main mast

Main mast

Mizzen mast

Holes for shrouds and backstays indicated by small dots

Bollards

Rigging leads (knots indicate which mast or sails can be controlled)

Rigging needs to be much longer than drawn, to extend well beyond bottle neck

Key to sail plan: *1 A jib topsail; 1 flying jib; 2 outer jib; 3 inner jib; 4 fore topmast staysail; 5 fore royal; 6 fore upper topgallant; 7 fore lower topgallant; 8 fore upper topsail; 9 fore lower topsail; 10 for course; 11 main royal staysail; 12 main topgallant staysail; 13 main topmast staysail; 14 main royal; 15 main upper top gallant; 16 main lower topgallant; 17 main upper topsail; 18 main lower topsail; 19 main course; 20 mizzen royal staysail; 21 mizzen topgallant staysail; 22 mizzen topmast staysail; 23 mizzen royal; 24 mizzen upper topgallant; 25 mizzen lower topgallant; 26 mizzen upper topsail; 27 mizzen lower topsail; 28 mizzen course (cro'jack); 29 jigger topgallant staysail; 30 jigger topmast staysail; 31 jigger staysail; 32 upper spanker; 33 lower spanker. In later days of sail the royal sails were omitted, partly for ease of handling by a smaller number of crew and economy on canvas. These barques were known as stump topgallant rig, and lend themselves ideally to putting into bottles.*

in mahogany was made for this model, stained and varnished; this adds an effective finishing touch. The four-masted barquentine has a hull 7¾ in long and with the bowsprit measures 9 in long overall.

These four-masted barquentines were handy vessels, for with the rigging being as it was only a small crew was needed and at the same time they were capable of carrying large cargoes. Many such ships were built just after the turn of the century, well-built in steel and more economical, from an owner's viewpoint, to run. There were many four-masted barquentines as well as quite a few five- and six-masted ones with many of them fitted with labour saving

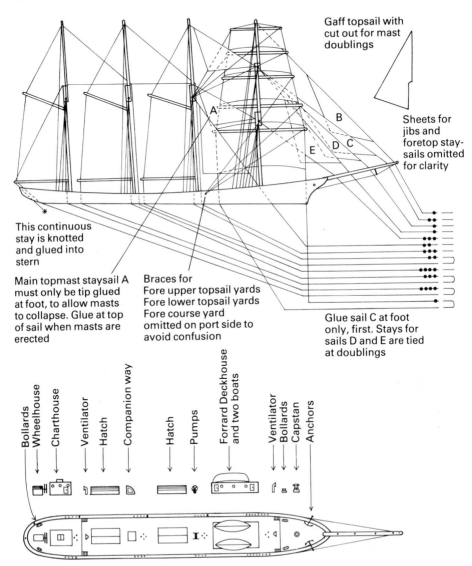

Gaff topsail with cut out for mast doublings

Sheets for jibs and foretop staysails omitted for clarity

This continuous stay is knotted and glued into stern

Main topmast staysail A must only be tip glued at foot, to allow masts to collapse. Glue at top of sail when masts are erected

Braces for
Fore upper topsail yards
Fore lower topsail yards
Fore course yard omitted on port side to avoid confusion

Glue sail C at foot only, first. Stays for sails D and E are tied at doublings

Bollards
Wheelhouse
Charthouse
Ventilator
Hatch
Companion way
Hatch
Pumps
Forrard Deckhouse and two boats
Ventilator
Bollards
Capstan
Anchors

Fig 26: *A four-masted barquentine, which is square rigged on the fore mast and fore and aft rigged on the main and jigger masts.*

The author's model of the four-masted barquentine (David Muscroft).

devices such as steam winches, which did take some of the toil out of sailing them.

One of my late pen friends told me of an amusing experience he had had whilst a crew-member on one of the bigger barquentines. After a long and exhausting trip from America to South Africa, their captain had been either unable or unwilling to pay the crew their overdue wages, so on his first trip ashore the crew sold the ship!

This type of ship makes an ideal model and is something a bit different from the stereotyped models you see in almost every nautical museum. I used $1/16$ in dowel throughout for the masts, yards and bowsprit, tapering in gradually for the upper masts. These dowels can be bought from a wholesale chemists (they are called 'applicators'), come in 6 in lengths in boxes of 144 and are ideal, as they are just that bit larger than the standard cocktail sticks. They were quite cheap, so since $1/16$ in dowels are hard to get, these filled the bill admirably, being made of straight-grained beech.

The diagram shows that the masts are drilled just above the doublings to take the continuous thread which is fastened at the stern. There is also an individual mast thread lead from each of the fore and aft rigged masts, all of which are a great help in a long bottle. The sheets which control the three jib sails and the fore topmast staysail are omitted from the diagram to avoid confusion, but these lead through ring bolts on the fo'c'sle to the forrard pin rails. Deckhouses, hatches and companion ways were made of beech, the ship's boats made as described in Chapter 10 and the capstan was made from a .177 lead airgun slug, filed down, but fitted to a pin to ensure that it was a firm fitting on the fo'c'sle deck. The ladders at the forrard end of the well deck and those leading to the poop deck were indicated by thin card marked with a fine black pen. The twin helms astern were two identical cogs from an old scrap pocket watch. The bold dots of the plan of the hull indicate the downhauls for the after end of the foot of the fore and aft sails. A substantial stand was made for this model from polished mahogany and a Turk's Head knot in fairly thick nylon line put an effective finishing touch to a model which, I feel, is a little out of the ordinary run-of-the-mill models.

Chapter 10

Other ship projects

A ship in a book

These are not so difficult as a ship in a bottle, are really effective and inevitably a surprise to visitors who browse through your bookshelf. Have a look through the contents of a secondhand bookshop and choose a book about 8 in × 5 in, with a nautical title. If you have an electric drill put eight $^1/_{16}$ in holes through the pages about $^1/_2$ in from the edges, holding the covers clear and making sure the pages are squarely together (see fig 27).

Then mark off about ten pages at a time and cut out the rectangle with a single edge razor blade until you have formed a 'box'. Next, stitch your pages together after glueing about every ten. The edges of the box and the bottom, ie, the back cover, should be painted pale blue, perhaps with a slight white cloud effect if you're good at painting, and a Plasticine sea can then be stuck into the bottom of the box and formed into waves. The ship is made similarly to a bottle model, but the masts are not hinged, they are simply fitted to holes in the deck. After your ship and glue have dried out, put a thick pane of celluloid or other transparent sheet over your box about $^1/_4$ in bigger all round, and stick this firmly down. Then another white sheet of paper the same size as your inside cover and front page should be cut, the latter with a rectangle the same size as the box formed for your ship. Glue all well down and there is your novelty model finished, to be admired by your friends.

Incidentally, this is an old smuggling trick adapted to a more honest purpose. They used to hollow out the old-fashioned Bibles, the ones with brass clasps,

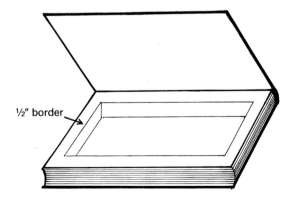

½″ border

Left, **Fig 27:** *Preparing a book to take a ship model.*

Above right *A model in a book provides a surprise for any visitor browsing through your book shelves!*

and perhaps put a flask of French brandy inside as well as jewellery. How long it was before the Excise men got wise to this is anyone's guess. Other miniatures can be made inside matchboxes and small electric light bulbs, but these latter are extremely fragile and call for great care when the brass cap is removed and the neck of the bulb cut off to take out the filament and inside parts.

Models in light bulbs

These are made on the same principle as bottle models but the sea must first be placed on a polythene base or similar sheet of material if you intend to make your model upright in the bulb. Secure the corners of the sheet with stout thread and after your model is erected and the excess thread from the rigging is cut off, pull the sea, with the model *in situ*, upright into the bulb, pulling out the sheet and building up the neck of the bulb with Plasticine of the same colour as the sea. Make sure there are no gaps visible from the outside. After leaving the model a few days to dry out, apply a good impact adhesive to the bulb neck and lamp cap and your model is ready to mount in a batten-type lamp holder.

These models are unusual, but they are all part of an enjoyable hobby, which offers much more of a sense of achievement than some others. They have the advantage of being permanent, and completely dustproof, and are always pleasing to the eye. Some inquisitive youngster will always ply you with endless questions about how you did it. Now you can tell them!

Scenic models

Made in a square Johnnie Walker whisky bottle, these are another modelling variation which really look well. The background of cliffs, woods, etc, can be made of Plasticine. First paint one side of your bottle (Darwin's satin finish is ideal), taking care not to mark the bottle neck. Only a *thin* coat of pale blue is necessary, with perhaps just a mere suggestion of white cloud. Lay the bottle flat until dry. You can make a beach of a strip of finest glass paper, and surround it with tiny fragments of coal which look like black wet rocks, while a jetty (see fig 28) is easily made from a half-inch section of wood with split matches glued vertically ⅛ in apart. The whole lot is painted matt black or brown with a little green at the waterline. One or two cottages can be carved from wood, and a tiny winding road down to the jetty or beach can be made of fine wet or dry paper strip. You can put in a tiny bridge with a stream made of silver paper beneath it, running down to the sea, and perhaps a windmill.

Windmills and other large-looking structures can be easily made from wood and incorporated into the background of scenic bottle models. The drawing shows the method of folding the sails. A pin is drilled through the centre of the sail beams and a hole drilled at an angle below the mill roof as shown at A. The sails are then folded like pair of scissors and once inside the bottle the pin is fixed into the hole drilled at an angle at A with a touch of adhesive then the sails adjusted to 90° before the adhesive dries.

The possibilities are endless, and your ship model is in the forefront, say a little brig or schooner putting out to sea. Always make sure your Plasticine is stuck on the background and pressed firmly. As a rule, though, it will hold on principally by its own weight apart from the fact that it will join up with your sea base. Naturally, a ship would not really sail as close in to land as this but that's where we are to be

You will find, of course, as I have, that you get asked some rather odd questions. I remember one dear old lady at a London exhibition who listened intently to my every word and examined the four-masted barque I had screwed

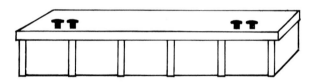

Fig 28: *A miniature jetty for scenic bottle models. (Not to scale.)*

Another example of how one can vary a model. This one is of the brig Marie Sophie, *which was particularly difficult to make as it has an* internal *stand as well as an external one. Also the model is not the usual waterline version but shows the whole of the hull. This was achieved by constructing the hull from three 'slices' (David Muscroft).*

on to the 8 in working base to keep the rigging taut. When some of the crowd had melted away to look at other attractions she said quietly, 'I understand how you fold up the masts and sails, young man' (I was eternally grateful for this, being in my early fifties!) 'but how do you get that long piece of wood in that short bottle?' Being as hoarse as one of the witches in *Macbeth*, after hours of talking, I mentally counted up to ten and croaked 'That piece of wood *doesn't* go in, my dear'. I still think she left in some doubt!

Minuscule ships in bottles

There are several ship-in-bottle makers in the world who take a great interest in making tiny models in bottles. Some of these are quite remarkable and I have seen two which even when placed end to end are not the length of a standard match. This branch of the hobby is one which requires exceptionally good eyesight, an immense amount of patience as well as a steady hand and a dainty touch. The smallest model ship I have ever made is $^5/_{32}$ in high and is encapsulated in a 13 amp glass fuse. The model is of a two-masted schooner of $^1/_4$ in long inside a fuse of $^{13}/_{16}$ in long. Of course at this scale any type of rigging is quite out of the question. I have built models such as these including two sailing ships in 2.5 V torch (flashlamp) bulbs as a 'gimmick' for various Exhibitions. Others were the result of direct challenges from people who bring me tiny perfume bottles deciding that these would have me 'stumped'. Actually quite a lot of impossible-looking models can be made, given enough incentive,

but I decided that, as far as I am concerned, the ship in the fuse is going to be my smallest!

I have made many small models to fit in the neck of a bottle along with a larger ship-in-bottle; sometimes as a replica of the larger ship. In these cases the masts and yards were made from very fine gauge wire, painted very *thinly* with stone coloured paint, (for every coat of paint increases the thickness and size of components); sails were made from thin white bank paper and the hulls of brass or some other soft metal filed to shape. At this scale a metal hull is preferable to wood for the edges look sharper and are not so susceptible to damage when handled in the making. Also the holes which have to be drilled for the masts and bowsprit are much more accurate, especially when the masts are inserted for there are of course no hinges at the foot. The masts, complete with sails, can quite often be placed in *en bloc* but if the bottle neck or aperture is only something like $3/32$ in the masts have to be put in first and the sails added on afterwards, (the sternmost mast being put in first followed by its sails and then the next mast and its sails, etc). Even at this scale though, it is possible to add deckhouses and ship's boats.

As with the larger ships-in-bottles the interior of the small bottle or bulb must be accurately measured and since the masts fit *into* the hulls, allowance must be made for a little clearance as the mast goes in at an angle and is pushed up into the near vertical position. Most masts did slope slightly towards the stern of a

ship and indeed some of the early American ships had an extreme rake. To make a model ship in a 2.5 V torch bulb, first obtain two identical bulbs as it is necessary to file the brass screw top from one bulb to get at the glass part; this must be done very gently as they are made of extremely thin glass. When the brass screw part has been removed you will be left with a glass bulb with a sealed pear-shaped end which is fastened to the filament on two wires. With a very fine file mark a groove round the base of the bulb to give an aperture of at least $1/8$ in. Then with the help of a little water or Brasso file gently into the groove, rotating the bulb in your fingers slowly to get a level and even cut. This is a rather tricky and fragile operation, but, with a gentle touch, there is little danger of the glass breaking in the wrong place. When the file has almost gone through the glass, snap off the bulb from the solid pear-shaped piece and finish off the cut edge of the bulb on a fine carborundum stone dampened with water. Wash out the inside of the bulb to remove all the powdered glass and wipe the inside dry with a tiny wad of cotton wool on the end of a cocktail stick. Allow to dry thoroughly.

Measure the outside diameter of the bulb and allowing $1/16$ in for the glass thickness, ($1/32$ in on each side) calculate the internal diameter. Then make a tiny drawing of the bulb shape, which may be either oval or round. If it is round the model ship can be made upright, with the brass screw cap above the top of the masts; if it is oval the ship can go in the same way as a full size ship goes into a bottle. Often there are bulbs which have become loose inside the brass cap and if you find one of these it's your lucky day, but, in any case, it is no hard matter to scrape out the cement which holds the bulb into the brass screw. Within the confines of the drawing, make a sketch of the type of ship you wish to build, say a two- or three-masted schooner, with the hull and bowsprit almost the length of the extreme diameter of the bulb for an upright model, (with an oval indicator-type bulb the hull can be a little longer). The height of a two-masted schooner is roughly $2/3$ of its overall length, ie, from extreme stern of hull to end of the bowsprit. The model two-masted schooner I made in a round bulb was $7/16$ in long overall and $5/16$ in high from the masthead to the bottom of the hull. This was mounted upright in the bulb, as mentioned previously. The model two-masted schooner in the oval bulb was $9/16$ in long overall and $11/32$ in high from the masthead to the bottom of the hull. The masts, as stated before, were made of fine wire, as was the bowsprit.

Cut the wire into 1 in lengths for painting and stick them into a blob of Plasticine to dry. Then cut to correct size, filing of the rough end which is to fit into the hull. The hull can be made by filing down a brass screw or from a scrap of aluminium but it should not be more than $3/32$ in wide or higher than $3/32$ in.

With a very small drill, the same size as the wire, drill the holes for the masts and bowsprit. It is better to drill the holes and insert masts before painting the hull else you may well ruin your paintwork. The deck can be painted first and then the hull which can be black, red or dark green (the usual colours for coastal schooners) or perhaps even dark brown, which was often a mixture of 'left-over' paints accumulated by a parsimonious owner. The bowsprit, which has been previously tapered at the forrard end, can then be fitted into the bows using a tiny dab of adhesive. Leave this to dry thoroughly. Tiny deckhouses can be made from good quality card, such as Bristol board or even white celluloid but this must not be more than $1/16$ in thick. The deckhouses can be left completely white or, alternatively, the roofs can be grey or black. The ship's boats can be made from small wheat seeds, carved from hardwood or can be made by using the method described in Chapter 6, using folded paper instead of metal. Obviously at this scale it is not possible to add too much detail but a wheelhouse and capstan can be added. One model I made a few years ago was in a Norman Hartnell *In Love* perfume bottle which was $1\,13/16$ in long $\times\,3/4$ in high $\times\,7/16$ in wide. The bottle neck aperture was just large enough to admit the head of a match. The bottle was painted light blue inside, with a mere touch of white for clouds and a tiny background strip of green Plasticine to represent 'land'. A brass end of a ball-point pen was used as a lighthouse painted white with red bands and embedded in tiny fragments of coal to give the impression of a lighthouse standing on rocks. A tiny windmill, also painted red and white, stands in the middle background with the lighthouse standing in the right hand corner of the bottle at the side of the neck. The ship is a four-masted schooner $7/8$ in long $\times\,7/16$ in high, has 12 sails and 3 deckhouses.

Another minuscule model, made in 1975, is the seven-masted schooner *Thomas W. Lawson*, in a perfume sample bottle $1\,3/8$ in long $\times\,5/16$ in high. The ship itself is $1\,1/16$ in long $\times\,1/4$ in high and has 18 sails. Two other models were made about the same time in Penicillin bottles, which are made of first class glass, thin and clear, which are, in fact, made in a similar manner to neon light tubes. The bottles were exactly 2 in long with a diameter of $13/16$ in and the bottle neck aperture was $5/16$ in which, compared with some of the others, is quite

A miniature model of the Charlotte Rhodes *(Sheffield Newspapers Limited, Sheffield).*

wide! A six-masted 'Great Lakes' schooner occupies one of these bottles with a red hull, stone coloured masts and bowsprit and 17 sails (a miniature of the big ship described in Chapter 8). The other bottle contains a tiny model of the *Charlotte Rhodes* which with black hull, buff painted deck, masts and bowsprit, green hatch covers and black roofed deckhouse, is a pleasing miniature replica of the large ship in the pint dimple bottle described in Chapter 4. The vessel is $^{15}/_{16}$ in long, $^1/_2$ in high and has 12 red/brown sails. Readers who have become fairly proficient at the hobby may care to make one of these models. They occasion some favourable comment, especially with the ladies!

Two more miniatures are in tiny dimple pattern bottles which are $1^7/_8$ in $\times$ $1^3/_8$ in (these bottles once contained a perfume called *Devonshire Violets*). These bottles have very narrow necks, into which a tiny rubber stopper fits possibly to prevent evaporation, of about $^1/_{16}$ in wide. Now, anyone who can get a ship through an aperture as tiny as that could possibly juggle with soot, but I am not so nimble fingered so I rounded off this aperture with a tiny pointed grindstone to $^3/_{16}$ in wide. This at least gave me a sporting chance. This grinding down operation was achieved by keeping the grindstone wet to avoid heat generation which would crack the bottle and to avoid inhaling glass dust (which is not conducive to longevity!). The bottle was then rinsed out and dried.

An approximate interior shape was obtained by rolling up a thin sheet of paper, inserting it into the neck of the bottle and flattening it out inside. Then, by continually withdrawing the paper and trimming it to fit, a fairly accurate shape was obtained. A miniature drawing of a clipper ship was made, scaling it down from a ship plan. The hull of a the ship was $1^1/_8$ in $\times$ $^5/_{32}$ in and with bowsprit the model was $1^3/_8$ in length overall and $^7/_8$ in high. The hull was made from a 1 1/2 in brass screw, filed down to the proper shape and three holes drilled for the masts and one in the bows for the bowsprit, which was made from a 1/2 in brass office pin. The fore and mizzen masts were 11/16 in long and the mainmast 13/16 in. The mainmast crossed six yards and the fore and mizzen five yards. There were, with staysails and jib sails, 26 sails in all. The masts, gaffs and yards were made from fine iron wire all painted stone colour to match the deck and bowsprit. Leaving all these 1 in long for painting, they were put into a blob of Plasticine to dry, filing them down and touching up with paint afterwards. Two deckhouses were made from card, the tops being painted black and a tiny wheelhouse added aft of the mizzen mast. This model was exhibited at the North American Exposition at San Diego in 1982.

The other dimple-type bottle was used for an even tinier 'Self-portrait' model than the one described in Chapter 15. This model shows a man seated on a four legged stool, with legs under a table 3/4 in long × 1/2 in wide × 3/8 in high. The man's figure was made with the trunk in three pieces while arms and legs were made from 1/16 in dowel, bent and glued as described for the larger figure. The table was made with the top in three sections, being hinged underneath with masking tape to enable it to fold up to go through the bottle neck, (it also had a strip of brown sealing paper stuck over the top when *in situ,* making all joints invisible). The model three-masted schooner on the table had an overall length of 13/16 in, was 3/8 in high and had 9 sails. There are tools on the table including a bradawl, saw and hammer; the hammer being made as described for the larger model and the saw was made from the finest gauge fretsaw, cut off with a handle added. As my hair is now more grey than brown I opted for a blob of white cotton wool for the figure's hair, in anticipation of the advancing years. In all there were 72 components.

I recently completed another small model of a three-masted schooner in one of those tiny brown tinted beer bottles which are available in wine stores. The bottles measures 3 5/16 in long with a diameter of 15/16 in. The one I chose was a Harp lager bottle for it is not as dark as the Guinness ones. The ship's hull was made from a brass screw, as in the previously explained model; the bowsprit from a 1/2 in brass office pin and masts and yards from thin wire, painted in a buff/stone colour. Most of the ships of the schooner era had masts finished in this colour, although occasionally some were varnished. American ships often

A miniature beer bottle model with stand.

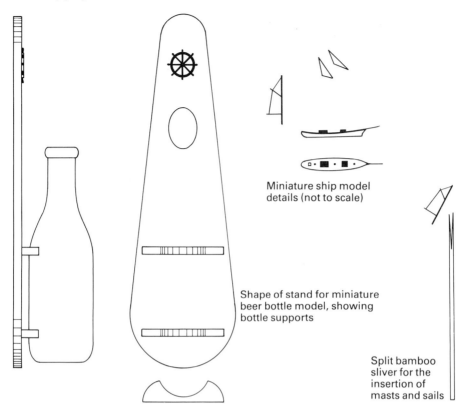

Miniature ship model
details (not to scale)

Shape of stand for miniature
beer bottle model, showing
bottle supports

Split bamboo
sliver for the
insertion of
masts and sails

Fig 29: *Plans for the construction of a ship model in a miniature beer bottle.*

had varnished masts, 'slushed' with grease to help hoist the mainsails. A small lighthouse was added to this model to add a touch of realism. The stand was an unusual shape with the tiny label from a miniature bottle stuck on the base, together with a miniature helm, purchased from a ship model shop. These tiny models occasion quite a lot of interest at exhibitions and the main question I get asked is 'Are these harder to make than the large ones?' Naturally, in some cases, they are harder to construct and so I find that two hours working on these miniatures is more than enough at any one time. Children of course are especially fascinated by tiny objects of any kind and the usual query from them is 'How much are they?' Obviously because such a lot of intricate work is entailed in these tiny models any craftsman is loath to part with them, but some have been donated to various museums. Personally I always keep a dozen miniatures for exhibition purposes, with some incorporated in the bottle neck of a larger model, as a replica and curiosity.

As always be careful in your choice of bottle. Avoid tiny bottles that are made of rather thick glass for these can spoil the effect of such a small model. The best receptacles are torch bulbs or Penicillin phials as the glass is thin and of a very high quality.

Chapter 11

Puzzle models

A simple puzzle model

The bottle chosen for this model is a miniature Warnink's Advocaat and, like many other wooden puzzles in bottles, at first glance the task looks quite impossible.

After the bottle has been cleaned and dried out, cut four lengths of hard wood, (preferably from wood without a pronounced grain, like sapele, satin walnut or beech) to 2 in long × ³⁄₈ in square. You will also need four chromium-

Fig 30: *A simple puzzle model incorporates four chromium-plated wood screws, and like so many bottle models looks 'impossible'.*

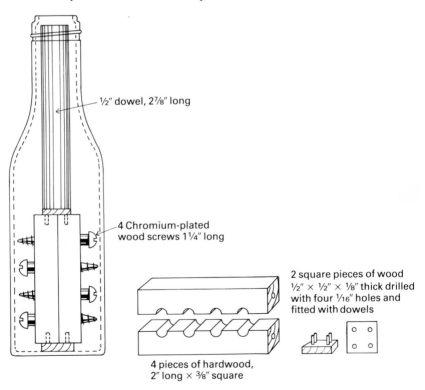

½" dowel, 2⅞" long

4 Chromium-plated wood screws 1¼" long

2 square pieces of wood ½" × ½" × ⅛" thick drilled with four ¹⁄₁₆" holes and fitted with dowels

4 pieces of hardwood, 2" long × ³⁄₈" square

A simple puzzle model for the beginner.

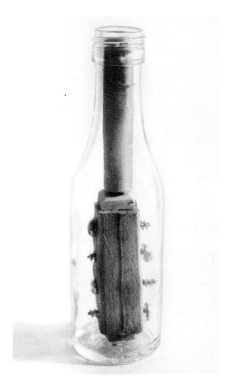

plated or brass screws of 1¼ in long. In each piece of wood cut four semi-circular grooves ½ in apart, and of a size to take the screws, making sure that they match up in pairs—it is best to number them to make sure. Place the matching pairs together and test for screw width, if necessary enlarge the holes slightly until the two pieces of wood fit so there is hardly any sign of a joint. Make sure that the four screws fit loosely—they should move sideways freely. Cut two squares of wood measuring ½ in square and ⅛ in thick and drill four ¹⁄₁₆ in holes in each. Glue four ¹⁄₁₆ in dowels in each piece, having drilled holes to receive these in the four 2 in long pieces, so the dowels act as locking pieces.

Securely glue the ½ in square dead centre of the bottle bottom and leave until quite dry. Insert one 2 in piece of wood with grooves into the centre of the bottle, with a dab of glue in the dowel hole. Next, put in the adjoining piece with a smear of glue at the side and press the two together. When completely dry, lower in the first screw on a loop of thread, followed by the other three. (The bottle of course is laid on its side for this operation.) Then put in the third 2 in piece of wood, followed by the last piece, with a smear of glue on the appropriate side. Then quickly place the top locking ½ in square to fix the whole structure together. With some accurate woodwork, the four joints should be hardly discernible, particularly if the wood has a fairly parallel grain.

The next stage is to cut a piece of ½ in dowel so it is 2⅞ in long. With a fairly sizeable blob of glue on the bottom end, this dowel is lowered in to the bottle so that it butts firmly on to the ½ in square. Place a steel rod on to the top of the dowel and wedge it firm; remove when the glue is set. When the puzzle is completely dried out the screws will move about from side to side if the bottle is

gently shaken. Leave for one, preferably two days to make sure it is completely
dry. Some molten sealing wax can be poured gently into the bottle neck, but
make sure none drips on to the dowel itself. This will seal the bottle
permanently. As one can see from the diagram, this is a fairly easy model to
make but it still looks quite impossible to the average layman. If preferred the
four wood pieces can be made longer and more screws put in, but try a simple
version like the one illustrated first!

A wooden cross in a bottle

This is a simplified version of one of the oldest types of models or puzzles in
bottles, which appear to have originated in Europe in the late 1700s or early
1800s. Some really beautifully decorated and highly skilful versions of the
cruxifixion were made during this period and La Musée des Arts et Traditions
Populaires in Paris has several wonderful examples. It is highly probable that
these models were made by monks or other people belonging to religious orders
as a hobby. The workmanship in these models is of a very high order indeed and
when the wooden joints are originally examined closely the viewer can be
excused for saying that 'It's impossible!' The model I will describe seems very
simple (and purposely so) when compared with some of these old masterpieces
and as all the ones I have seen bear no name, one can only admire these
craftsman of the past and strive to emulate their unique standard of
workmanship.

The wooden cross I constructed was made in beech and measures $2^7/8$ in high
by $2^3/4$ in wide. In section it is $1/2$ in $\times$ $11/16$ in and it stands on a wooden base
which measures 2 in $\times$ $7/16$ in $\times$ $1/4$ in. The bottle I used, which is in the region
of 100 years old, was given to me by a friend who spends his leisure time
'digging' on the sites of forgotten villages for antique glass bottles. [This is a
very lucrative pastime for rare perfume bottles, purple poison bottles and Codd
bottles—the ones which were sealed with a glass ball—are all quite valuable if in
good condition.] Of course most of these old bottles have several surface
scratches and flaws and often the neck of the bottle is not straight. However,
this particular bottle was 'tailor made' for a wooden puzzle type of model. The
dimensions of the wooden cross sections are therefore only applicable to a bottle
of similar size (this bottle was $5^1/4$ in $\times$ $3^1/8$ in $\times$ $1^5/16$ in) and naturally if you
can get an antique bottle with a slightly larger neck aperture, then the model
cross can be proportionately larger or wider in section.

The upright part of the cross consists of four sections, as does the horizontal
part. The $1/16$ in dowels which hold the eight sections of the cross together
cannot, of course, be seen in the finished model. The four upright sections of
the cross are further secured by being morticed into the wooden base. Since this
flask-shaped bottle, which many decades ago would probably have contained
brandy or whisky, had been buried for a long time in the ground it was
necessary to clean it as thoroughly as possible both inside and out. So the inside
was filled with warm water and a strong solution of bleach added and allowed to
stand immersed in a container filled with the same solution for 48 hours. A
small blob of cotton wool was bound on to a stout wire with thread and the
more persistent stains removed whilst the bleach solution was still in the bottle.
This method proved very effective and the bottle ended up remarkably clean in
view of its long sojourn in the ground. Many of the superficial scratches were
impossible to eradicate, but this did not detract too greatly and in fact imparted

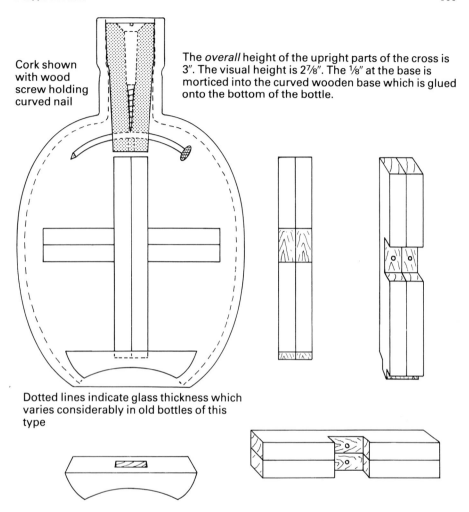

Cork shown with wood screw holding curved nail

The *overall* height of the upright parts of the cross is 3″. The visual height is 2⅞″. The ⅛″ at the base is morticed into the curved wooden base which is glued onto the bottom of the bottle.

Dotted lines indicate glass thickness which varies considerably in old bottles of this type

Fig 31: *Diagrams for a wooden cross. This is a simplified version of one of the oldest types of models or puzzles in a bottle.*

an old world look to what was a new model. As before warm tap water was run into the bottle and after drying out a quantity of surgical spirit was swished around to complete the cleaning process.

As can be seen from the diagram the four upright sections of the cross have a cross-lap joint cut into them, 1 in from the top and ½ in wide, to accommodate two of the horizontal sections. The easiest way to make this joint is to cut two parallel lines ½ in apart with a fine saw. Cut half way through the wood section and then carefully remove the wood from between the cuts with a small wood-carver's chisel, finishing off with a file and fine glasspaper. The upright and cross sections should be 'matched' together and, again, it is a good plan to number each half of the joint with its fellow. The reason for this precaution will be readily apparent as all joints are not necessarily uniform, unless the modeller is exceptionally good at joinery!

So, you will now be left with two pairs of uprights and two pairs of horizontal sections. The cross-lap joints should be checked now for a completely flush fitting as the four pieces, when assembled, form half the cross. When these are 'sandwiched' together they should form a reasonably solid-looking cross comprised of eight sections in all. The more accurate the workmanship the more solid and convincing the finished cross will appear. The bottom parts of the four upright sections, which fit into the mortice in the wooden base, must now be cut $^{1}/_{4}$ in from the end. The mortice in the base of this particular model was $^{1}/_{2}$ in $\times$ $^{1}/_{8}$ in. The simplest method of making this joint is to drill three holes with a $^{1}/_{8}$ in drill, then join these up with the aid of a small chisel and file to form a mortice slot $^{1}/_{2}$ in $\times$ $^{1}/_{8}$ in, so that in section the upright ends will be $^{1}/_{2}$ in $\times$ $^{1}/_{16}$ in when placed side by side.

The shape for the wooden base was determined by laying on a sheet of tracing paper over the bottle and marking the arc of the curve. If the bottle you have obtained has a flat base, so much the better. It is not absolutely vital to make the wooden base a perfect fit to the sides of the bottle but the fitting at the base is an important factor as this ensures the cross is perfectly vertical. At this point and before the application of glue dries the base must be tested for alignment by inserting two of the upright sections in the bottle (one at a time!) and adjusting the seating of the wooden base on the bottom of the bottle. The mortice joint must not be a 'forced' fit but the upright sections should fit in easily and smoothly with just a fraction of 'tolerance', (for remember four upright sections have to fit in the mortice).

When you are completely satisfied that the eight sections of the cross fit snugly in their respective joints the $^{1}/_{16}$ in holes can be drilled to accommodate the dowels. These holes must be drilled through only half the thickness of the wood otherwise they will mar the look of the finished model. The way to ensure that you do drill only halfway through is to measure the wood and if, for example, it is $^{1}/_{2}$ in thick the hole must only be $^{1}/_{4}$ in deep. So, bind a small length of black adhesive tape round the drill $^{1}/_{4}$ in from the end then you can see when you get to the required depth. These dowels only act as a positive positioning device and are, of course, used in conjunction with the adhesive. If desired the cross can be coated with polyurethane varnish, but leave bare the sides which are to be fastened together. Varnishing is not essential but it does act as a preservative and brings out the grain of the wood. However, do bear in mind the advice given elsewhere in the book about varnish and paint adding slightly to the size of the components.

It is a good idea to round off the ends of the dowels in the uprights slightly as this helps enormously later on when assembling the cross in the bottle. Finally, assemble all the sections together for a final check and if any of the sections do not quite line in the assembled position, rub the area down with a sheet of finest glasspaper. Now the cross is ready to be placed in the bottle. The morticed base is the first to go in then the first upright section should be lightly dabbed with a slow-drying adhesive and placed in position, following as quickly as possible with the upright section which fits at the side of it. Then the bottom one of the horizontal pieces is fitted, again with just a dab of adhesive and pressed firmly into position, followed by the corresponding top piece. Having now placed half the cross in the bottle, recheck for alignment and leave for a while to set. Then repeat the procedure for the other side, putting a *thin* overall coat of adhesive on the two upright sections where they fit back-to-back with the first half of the

A wooden cross in a bottle. Note the added feature of a curved nail piercing the cork (see fig 31 and text for details).

cross. Do not make the mistake of putting too much adhesive on the surface or this will exude from the joints and made the finished product rather unsightly. You can now leave the cross for a good few hours to dry out and form a good solid fixture.

When the reader is on an odd visit to various museums which have ships-in-bottles in their collections, some 'sailor-made' models may be seen which have the cork pierced on the *inside* of the bottle with a straight or curved nail or dowel. To the layman this appears impossible but like many complicated types of puzzles, this has a comparatively simple explanation and, in point of fact, there are at least *three* ways in which this can be achieved! When you think of a cork going into a bottle you quite naturally think of it being *forced* in, so you have to reverse this train of thought and sand down an appropriate cork so that it will *drop* into the bottle, not so it is too slack a fit but one which will drop in (and out!) of the bottle neck.

So, having found the requisite cork, (preferably one which has not been damaged by a corkscrew) drill a $\frac{1}{8}$ in hole at the top, making sure that the hole is central. But only drill halfway through and then drill again, this time from the bottom, to meet the first hole, running the drill through a couple of times to clear out any pieces of loose cork. Then find a suitable nail with a diameter of about $\frac{1}{8}$ in and enough length to go through the cork horizontally and protrude at each side of the cork. The masonry type nails are best as these are usually of a rust-free alloy. Drill a hole the same diameter as the nail horizontally through the cork and enlarge the hole slightly. It is not necessary for the nail to be a tight fit because, as will be explained later, it is 'locked' into position. Then select a wood screw with a flat head, which, when screwed into the cork, will serve the dual purpose of locking the nail in position and also 'swelling' the cork so that it is a tight fit in the bottle. Countersink the top of the cork so that when the screw is in position it will be flush with the cork top and will also lightly bear on the nail. As previously stated there are at least three ways of putting a nail through the cork on the inside of a bottle so it would perhaps be better if I describe the simplest method first.

Cut a thin slot with a razor blade across the bottom of the cork to meet the horizontal hole and cut a not too obvious bevel alongside each side of the slot. Then, measuring the bottom width of the cork, file the part of the nail which will afterwards be drawn up into the cork to an inverted V shape. The reason for this is that, when the thread which is inserted through the vertical hole in the cork to draw up the nail into its horizontal position, the V section opens up the slot in the cork allowing the nail to fit snugly into the hole drilled to accommodate it and the bottom of the cork closes of its own accord, thus giving the illusion of 'impossibility'. A length of thread 10 in long is looped with two turns around the middle of the nail and the thread ends taken up through the bottom of the cork and temporarily held by means of a paper clip. It helps at this stage to put a small blob of glue on the V section of the nail to act as a lubricant when the nail is pulled upwards through the hole in the cork, as well as securing it in its proper position. Then the nail is dropped into the bottle neck. Holding the two ends of the thread tightly, lower the nail with the cork until it stops swinging, then pull the cork back up into the bottle neck and ease the nail into the horizontal slot. When it is in position, pull the cork up a little further out of the bottle neck and hold it temporarily with a stout pin inserted horizontally whilst you pull on *one* of the threads to draw it away from the nail.

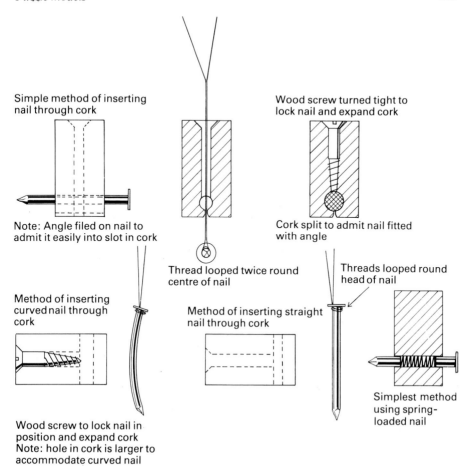

Simple method of inserting nail through cork

Note: Angle filed on nail to admit it easily into slot in cork

Wood screw turned tight to lock nail and expand cork

Cork split to admit nail fitted with angle

Thread looped twice round centre of nail

Threads looped round head of nail

Method of inserting curved nail through cork

Method of inserting straight nail through cork

Simplest method using spring-loaded nail

Wood screw to lock nail in position and expand cork
Note: hole in cork is larger to accommodate curved nail

Fig 32: *The three methods of inserting a nail through the cork. A full description is given in the text.*

Care should be exercised at this point to avoid moving the nail out of position. Then the wood screw can be inserted and screwed into position, to 'lock' the nail. The top of the screw can be covered in sealing wax and then the modeller can stand back and wait to answer such questions as 'How on earth did you do that?'

There are two or more ways to put nails through corks and this next one is the most professional and understandably the more difficult. However, this next method can only be used when there is a fair amount of space to manoeuvre between the model and the bottle neck. The same two holes are drilled as before but with the horizontal holes slightly bigger than previously and no slot is cut in the bottom of the cork. In this instance the nail is given two or three turns of looped thread near its *head* and the wood screw is given one or two turns into the hole in the top of the cork to provide a hand hold on it. Now comes the rather difficult part when the nail is, of course, hanging point downwards. At this point the bottle is best laid on its side whilst the nail is 'jiggled', (for want of a more precise word!) into the horizontal (when the bottle is upright) hole in the cork. This positioning of the nail takes some little time and patience. Immediately the nail is centrally placed in the cork pull gently on one end of the thread, having first removed the wood screw for the moment; then replace the screw and turn to lock the nail securely. Although this method is understandably more difficult to execute it certainly baffles even the more acute observer. If a curved nail is preferred, the horizontal hole must be drilled a trifle larger and the method just described is a little more difficult, but you will find this a challenge you cannot resist! Finish off the same way as before with sealing wax.

The last method is comparatively simple and consists of a nail cut in two and joined by a fine spring, such as can be found in electric light fittings. Only a few coils of the spring are needed and the two ends of the nail, when the coil spring is compressed, must be no wider than the bottle neck aperture. The operation must be executed quickly for the spring, which is, of course, securely attached to the two ends of the nail, has to be coated with adhesive. So no time can be lost or else the spring may not expand to force out the ends of the nail into the inside width of the bottle.

Chapter 12

First figure models in bottles

A fisherman

The bottle chosen for this model is a one pint Burnett's gin bottle, oval in section and made from tinted green glass. It is 10 in × 3³/₄ in × 2⁵/₈ in.

The two halves of the figure's body section are carved in beech wood which, in section, are 4¹/₈ in × ³/₄ in. These measurements are, of course, dependent on the diameter of the bottle neck, which in this case is just slightly over ³/₄ in. Should the bottle of your choice have a wider neck aperture than this then the figure can be made correspondingly 'fuller'. The two sections at A and B are united by beech dowels as indicated and, between the thick arrowed sections shown in the diagram, should be dead flat and a perfect fit. The leg sections are shaped round to represent seaboots with the aid of a file and glasspaper and drilled at points C, D, G and H to receive ¹/₁₆ in dowels. Paint a white undercoat to where jersey will end and the leg section in matt black. The two upright holes in the neck and shoulder section are drilled to accept two dowels in the head which also help to lock the two body pieces together (C). These dowels should not be a tight fit as they merely act as positioning pegs and aid jointing, which is where a slow-drying adhesive is used. These sections should be constantly checked for bottle neck clearance *together with dowels* and suitable allowance made for the fisherman's 'jersey' which was, in this case, made from Scholl's finger bandage. This type of bandage is an ideal medium to represent a white wool jersey and should be applied slightly damp on top of a thin coat of adhesive after the initial white paint has dried. Remember to slightly recess body sections at the shoulders as this gives 'spread' to the arms. When dry, trim off the excess bandage where it overlaps the two arrowed flat sections. The reasons for applying the bandage damp are twofold, as any wrinkles can be easily smoothed out and when it is dry the material tightens. It can then be given one or two coats of Humbrol matt white paint. The collar and cuffs as well as the seaboot stocking tops and the jersey hem are made separately by rolling up the bandage on the finger and glueing it well to form a convincing thickness of material. The two rolls can now be fitted to the leg portions but be sure to test for bottle neck clearance before painting.

The arms are made from ³/₈ in dowel, angled at the elbows (E) to suit the width of the bottle. The right and left arms should be rounded where they will unite with the body sections (D), which are slightly recessed, and these are drilled at the shoulder ends for dowels as well as at the elbows. Again the elbow sections should be dead flat and as perfect a fit as possible. Paint matt white.

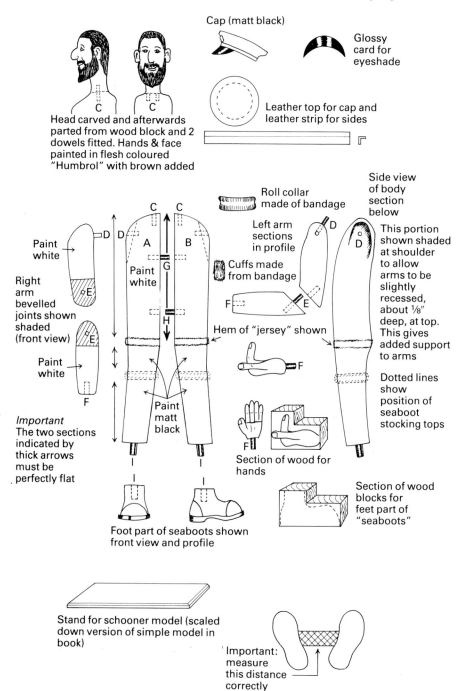

Cap (matt black)

Glossy card for eyeshade

Leather top for cap and leather strip for sides

Head carved and afterwards parted from wood block and 2 dowels fitted. Hands & face painted in flesh coloured "Humbrol" with brown added

Roll collar made of bandage

Side view of body section below

Paint white

Right arm bevelled joints shown shaded (front view)

Paint white

Important
The two sections indicated by thick arrows must be perfectly flat

Paint white

Paint matt black

Left arm sections in profile

Cuffs made from bandage

Hem of "jersey" shown

This portion shown shaded at shoulder to allow arms to be slightly recessed, about ⅛" deep, at top. This gives added support to arms

Dotted lines show position of seaboot stocking tops

Section of wood for hands

Section of wood blocks for feet part of "seaboots"

Foot part of seaboots shown front view and profile

Stand for schooner model (scaled down version of simple model in book)

Important: measure this distance correctly

Fig 33: *The diagrams are for a fisherman model but the components are standard to all figures, with little variation.*

Then, once dry, cover these with damp bandage as used for the body sections, trimming off any excess where the arms are to be jointed. Paint the same way as for the body sections. The feet part of the seaboots are made by cutting two L-shaped sections from a block of beech, which are then cut and filed to the profile shape of the boots. Then round off the toecap and ankle with a file and fine glasspaper until you can see them assume the shape of nautical footwear. The sole and heel can be filed in carefully and the front part of the boot scored where the toecap is, the heel re-inforcement can be similarly scored. The two completed 'feet' parts of the boots are then drilled to take the dowels from the bottom of the leg section (I).

The modeller may be dubious as to his ability to carve intricate parts like the head, face and hands, in which case a practice on a few scraps of softwood is beneficial. For easy handling do as much carving and finishing as possible before cutting the head or hands from the main length of wood. Use the diagrams in this chapter as a general guide to any model heads you may wish to make. Finish shaping with a file, then with glasspaper and, if possible, a dentist's 'burr' (ask your dentist for any old ones he may have for these will still be sharp enough for woodworking). The mouth can be formed by drilling a series of holes with a $1/32$ in drill and then joining these up with a scalpel. If you are going to use celluloid or sheet ivory for teeth or eyes—and I personally feel these give the best effect—the mouth has to be made a little wider than normal. The head, face and hands should be painted with Humbrol flesh-coloured paint with just a trace of red and brown to give the fisherman that 'weathered' look.

When the paint is completely dry, drill two holes at each side of the neck underside for dowels, making sure that these are wide enough apart to accommodate each side of the body section at the neck (C). Insert the dowels with a smear of adhesive and leave $3/16$ in protruding. The 'hair' on the model was made by laying of black, brown or grey Silko a few strands at a time and trimming them off at the forehead once the adhesive was dry. (This method, although taking a little more patience and time, looks far more effective than matt paint.) The hands of course are particularly delicate to carve especially when forming the fingers and so require a little extra care. The hands must be cut with the finest saw blade you can obtain and there are small saws used by watchmakers and jewellers which are ideal for small work like this and are a worthwhile investment for the modeller. The hands for this model must be formed with the fingers at 90° to the palms to 'hold' the model ship, so start with two L-shaped pieces of beech with the grain of the wood running as shown in the diagram. Shape hands as realistically as possible, leaving the sawing between the fingers until last. Support the model hand firmly between your thumb and forefinger whilst sawing, but be careful not to saw your own hand! If desired, the knuckles and nails can be indicated with score lines using a file or scalpel, for little details like this add a touch of realism. The top of the hands at the wrist part can now be drilled and the $1/16$ in dowels inserted with a touch of adhesive (F), but do not glue to the arms yet. Then paint these with the paint left over from the face. When this is dry assemble to test for clearance in the bottle neck.

The collar of the seaman's jersey can be fitted just below the chin on the head section and test this too for bottle neck clearance. This is then glued on to the body and the collar carefully painted white. This forms the jersey collar and also helps to cover the dowel joints.

Now assemble the complete figure—*but do not glue yet!* Test all dowels for fitting and see that the joints at the wrists and ankles are as perfect as possible and that the matt black of the legs blends into the black of the seaboots with the least hint of a join as possible. Your model figure should now stand upright. I found that by adjusting the feet so that they pointed outwards slightly gave the figure added stability. Take a piece of thin card, a postcard is ideal, and trace the outline of the seaboots and their distance apart. Be meticulous in this operation as this will be the guide for the position of your figure when it is placed in the bottle, and as the feet go in first it is upon these that the accuracy of the figure depends. Cut the card to the shape shown in the diagram. The shaded part between the feet will have a coat of sand when in the bottle, but none must go on the 'footprints' or the feet will not adhere firmly to form a solid 'anchor' for your figure.

With all figure models ample time must be allowed for every joint to dry out and all moisture allowed to evaporate from the bottle. If the modeller rushes the result will be a mixture of mildew and condensation which is extremely difficult, if not impossible, to eradicate once the model is finished. Also, in the case of this particular model, bear in mind that the feet part of the seaboots have to support the *whole figure firmly* as well as the added weight of the model ship held in the fisherman's hands. So, test the soles of the boots for fitting on the base of the bottle where the guide card is positioned and, if necessary, file or glasspaper them down slightly to achieve a good fit. Most bottles of this type are slightly convex at the base, so take this into consideration when drill holes are made in the feet for dowelling. When you are completely satisfied that all the various components fit together snugly and accurately and that there are no untidy threads hanging, etc, assemble the figure again—still no glue—for a final testing. Round off the ends of all dowels slightly and make certain that the hands will be perfectly level to hold the model ship.

The fisherman's cap and his beard are optional but they do add an extra touch of authenticity and are not difficult to make. The cap can be made by cutting a thin piece of leather into a circle for the top. The sides of the cap are made of a long strip of the same material. The best thing to use for the cap is the soft tongue of an old black shoe or part of a leather wallet. Thin the leather down with a scalpel or sharp craft knife. The length of the side strip of leather depends, of course, on the circumference of the cap top but allow at least $1/8$ in for the join, which should be made at the front of the cap and then covered by a small circular 'gold' badge with an anchor motif, (one of those cigarette packets made of gold-foil-covered card is ideal). Score the strip of leather with the back of a thin knife to form an L-section; the shortest bar of the L joins the underneath part of the cap top. Glue the underneath part of the cap top and when the glue is 'tacky' form the angled strip of leather round the edge. A small coin or cork can be used to keep this circular until the glue sets. The top of the cap can then be bent slightly concave to give it a well-worn look. The peak of the cap can be made from a glossy piece of thin black card, which again can be made from a cigarette packet. Cut this to fit the front of the cap and bend to the shape in the diagram.

Now you can insert the 'footprints' card, having first given the base of the bottle a coating of glue. (A thick coat is advisable here.) The card will have to be inserted in the bottle in the form of a roll and positioned with the heels almost at the back of the bottle since the arms of the figure project well forward. The hem of the fisherman's jersey can touch the back of the bottle for this helps to give the figure added stability. When the 'footprints' are securely stuck to the base of the bottle apply glue to the shaded part of the card *only* and to the rest of the bottle base. This can be easily done by using an ordinary child's paint brush made longer by pushing the handle into a small diameter plastic tube or into a length of ¼ in dowel in to which a hole has been bored, both enable you to reach the base of the bottle. Another coat of glue should be applied and a quantity of fine dry sand, such as is found in egg-timers, distributed over the bottom of the bottle to cover it completely. The easiest way to do this is to get a length of plastic or metal tubing 6 in × ¼ in and make a paper funnel. Tape the funnel securely to the top of the tube and it is then comparatively simple to pour in a small quantity of sand, moving the tube in a circular motion. Shake the sand gently about so it covers the base of the bottle thinly. Be as careful as possible while you are doing this since fine sand tends to cling to the sides of the bottle and can scratch when it is being removed. So, do not put in any more sand than is absolutely necessary. Excess sand can be wiped off the sides by lying the bottle on its side and using a wad of damp cotton wool fastened to a wire. Do this as *gently* as possible.

Then give the two 'footprints' a good coat of adhesive and when it is tacky place in the feet of the figure. This can be achieved with a length of ⅛ in dowel with the last ⅜ in reduced to 1/16 in diameter. Use this to wedge into the dowel hole of the feet and then lower them into position on to the glue; press them well down. Another length of dowel can be pressed on to the toecap to release the fixing dowel and to adjust the feet into the *exact* position. Leave for at least 24 hours and remember not to rush on to the next stage.

When the feet have firmly stuck to the base—if in any doubt test for movement—lay the bottle on its side and insert one half of the body section. Then place in the other half, lightly coated with adhesive. Again, be careful not to overdo the adhesive or the excess will ooze out of the joins. Press the two halves of the figure together and then, resting the figure on the back of the bottle put a drop of adhesive in each dowel hole in the feet. Ease the figure into place and press in lightly. Righten the bottle. Then before the adhesive has a chance to set, lower in the head, which is complete with collar, on a *fixed* loop of string, (not a slip knot) which you can pass under the chin; put a spot of adhesive on the two neck dowels first and press firmly into position. This, together with the dowels pressed into the feet will lock the body parts together. Allow 24 hours to dry out.

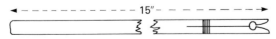

Fixing gadget made from bamboo cane, split
and bound with fuse wire

The *upper* arms can now be attached. The easiest way to do this is to get a piece of bamboo garden cane about 6 in × ⅛ in × 1/16 in and split up its length about 2 in. [This easy-to-make gripping tool is ideal for fitting on arms and legs of any figure inside a bottle, and is invaluable to the modeller.] Use this bamboo 'fork' to pick up the arm and lower carefully until it rests just in the shoulder hole. With a wire held in your other hand put a small dab of adhesive on the dowel and on the inside of the armpit. If desired the adhesive can be added first, but care must be taken not to stick the bamboo to the dowel! Then press the arm into the dowel socket and shoulder recess. Repeat for the other arm and again allow plenty of time to dry.

The hands can now be joined to the wrist parts but *not* yet glued. The reason for this is that when the elbow join is made the hands may need canting slightly to form a level platform for the ship's stand. To fix the forearm and hands, wind a piece of thread about 12 in long around where you would judge the point of balance to be, testing this to see that it does in fact hang level. When you are satisfied on this point apply the adhesive to both dowel and bevelled surface, tilt and lower through bottle neck until the dowel is opposite the hole at the elbow. With a length of dowel press it into place, whilst still holding the thread in your other hand. Repeat this procedure with the other arm and then leave to dry for 24 hours.

When the elbow joints are completely dry, move the hands to matching horizontal positions and before pressing into place put a small amount of adhesive on each dowel; again leave to dry. The fisherman's cap can now be put into position having first put a liberal coat of adhesive inside and round the brim. Press firmly on to the figure's head and adjust to a jaunty angle to add a swaggering air.

The ship model, is a comparatively simple model and it is the modellers personal choice whether to do a two- or three-masted schooner as the finishing touch to the fisherman model. The methods of constructing two- or four-masted schooners are fully described in the Chapters 3 and 4. Naturally the measurements of model must be scaled down to suit this particular figure model.

The stand for the ship model was made from a strip of beech $2^{1}/_{4}$ in $\times$ $^{7}/_{16}$ in $\times$ $^{1}/_{16}$ in with the edges bevelled and two coats of polyurethane varnish for a finished look. A small quantity of blue Plasticine is moulded into a 'sea' with minute quantities of white added to represent wave crests and the wake. The area of Plasticine where the hull of the ship model will rest should be recessed to $^{1}/_{8}$ in to give the model a secure 'seabed' and to hold it firmly in position.

Inserting the ship into the bottle is a little more difficult than putting a ship in a bottle in the horizontal position, because the masts have to be partially erected as soon as the model ship is clear of the bottle neck. This can be done by holding the bowsprit with a fairly large pair of tweezers. The model can then be held by a hooked wire placed under one of the mast stays (top of the mast) and the model is then pressed into the Plasticine 'sea'. A small blob of adhesive can be put in the hull depression in the sea if desired, but use slow drying adhesive and erect the rigging tightly before the adhesive sets. A long dowel with a flat edge is the best gadget to use for this, but do not use an undue amount of pressure, remembering that the fisherman is having to take the strain. When the rigging is completely taut embed the ends of the excess rigging into the 'sea' temporarily and apply minute blobs of adhesive at the four points where the rigging passes through the bowsprit. Leave for a good period to dry. Then, cut off the excess rigging under bowsprit and hide all the remainder under the 'sea'. Leave the model for at least a week to dry out before permanently fixing in the cork.

Right *Model of a fisherman with a ship in his hands.*

List of necessary materials
An empty Burnett's gin bottle
One length of beech, 12 in × 1 in × ³/₄ in (for head and two body sections)
¹/₁₆ in dowel or cocktail sticks
12 in length of ¹/₄ in dowel
12 in length of ³/₈ in dowel (for arms)
Scholl's finger bandage, tubular (sold in box containing one roll)
One length beech, 6 in × 1¹/₂ in × ¹/₂ in (for hands and feet)
Reel of Silko, colour to suit, for hair and beard of figure
Slow drying adhesive—Copydex or latex-based adhesive
Humbrol paint in white (matt), black (matt), flesh colour, red and brown
Small quantity of cotton wool
Small quantity of fine sand
Piece of thin black leather, about 4 in × 3 in
Thin card, a postcard is ideal. Also gilt and glossy black card
¹/₄ in metal or plastic tube, 10 in long if possible
A jeweller's fine saw or blade
A couple of long wires, about 10 in × ¹/₈ in (diameter)
A length of bamboo cane about 10 in long

Materials for the ship model
Cocktail sticks for masts
Chinese toothpicks for yards
Bond paper for sails
Brown or black Sylko for rigging
Humbrol paint, colours to choice, suggest green, black or red for hull of ship
Blue and white Plasticine for 'sea'
Beech strip, 2¹/₂ in × ⁷/₁₆ in × ¹/₁₆ in (for stand)

Long John Silver
The same rules apply to this figure as to the fisherman, so it is wise to read the previous section before attempting this one.

This model was an instance of the bottle inspiring the model, which was 'dreamed up' when this most unusual bottle, unfortunately empty, was sent to me by a pen-friend from Brisbane. It had previously contained rum. The bottle, which measures 7¹/₂ in × 4¹/₄ in × 2¹/₂ in, has 18th century sailing ships actually embossed in the glass and this unusual feature alone lent itself to a model of this kind, so what better subject could there be than the rascally sea-cook immortalised in Robert Louis Stevenson's *Treasure Island* (indeed one of the glass embossed ships on the bottle could well have been the *Hispaniola*!) *Treasure Island* has long been a favourite book of mine and one which I never tire of reading. Knowing full well, however, that such a bottle must be a rarity in this country—I have never seen another like it—it must be appreciated that the size of the components described will have to be modified to suit a different size bottle. However, if a clear glass wine decanter of comparable size can be found this would be ideal.

Right, Fig 34: *The figure of Long John Silver gives the reader another idea for a bottle model.*

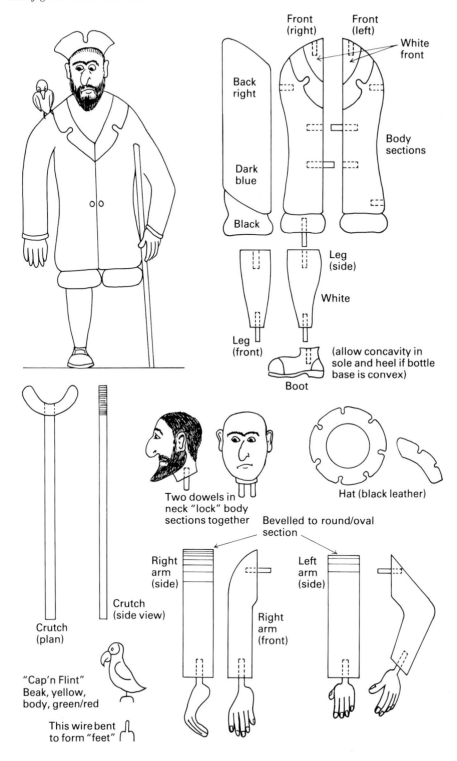

Front (right)

Front (left)

White front

Back right

Dark blue

Black

Body sections

Leg (side)

White

Leg (front)

Boot

(allow concavity in sole and heel if bottle base is convex)

Crutch (plan)

Crutch (side view)

Two dowels in neck "lock" body sections together

Bevelled to round/oval section

Hat (black leather)

"Cap'n Flint" Beak, yellow, body, green/red

This wire bent to form "feet"

Right arm (side)

Right arm (front)

Left arm (side)

Long John Silver and his parrot 'Cap'n Flint' from Treasure Island'.

The main purpose for the inclusion of this section is to give the reader another idea for a figure model. As with the fisherman model previously described the wood used for the figure itself was beech, thin black leather for the hat and sheet ivory or white celluloid for the teeth and eyes. Flesh-coloured Humbrol paint was used for the face and hands, but with a touch of brown paint added to give the skin a tanned look. The trunk of the body which is mostly jacket, was painted in dark blue matt almost down to the knees, with the exception of a white shirt front, and the lapels were indicated by means of the thread and pin method described in the Domino Players model (see Chapter 16). Two brass buttons on the jacket were made of minute brass screws with the head filed down flat and given a coat of varnish to prevent discolouration. Below the jacket the breeches were painted matt black.

Now, putting a standing figure of a man in a bottle is never easy, so it can be imagined that a one legged man does tend to present added difficulties. But, nevertheless, I found this model to be a fascinating challenge and perhaps my former experiences as a seaman, when I was often called upon to help an inebriated colleague back on board, was of some assistance in keeping the figure of Long John Silver in a vertical plane! His 'real' leg was painted in matt white to represent a stocking and his shirt front was painted in the same colour. His one shoe was painted in gloss black and a silver buckle was taken from a tiny watch strap for a shoe decoration. Although Long John Silver has been wonderfully portrayed in countless films and television series by the late and unforgettable Robert Newton as a dark haired man, he was, according to Robert Louis Stevenson, a blond man with a beard, so this is how he has been portrayed in my model. With a rough wooden crutch under his left armpit, a suitable villainous expression and his parrot, Cap'n Flint, perched on his shoulder one can almost imagine the cries of 'Pieces of eight' being screeched by this roguish bird. The latter was also carved from a scrap of beech, painted in red and green, with a yellow beak. His legs were made of fine iron wire and fitted into two small holes drilled in Long John's shoulder.

The base of the bottle was covered by a small sheet of fine glasspaper, cut to shape and glued firmly down, to represent a sandy shore, with a small amount of Plasticine to give an effect of an edge of grass into which were stuck a few small plants, (which were bought from a toy shop and being of a green plastic material are immune to fading). These plants cost only a few pence and are, in fact, model farmyard accessories.

The diagram illustrating this model should be self-explanatory and the methods of construction given for other figure models in this book apply equally to Long John Silver. Make especially sure that the figure, when assembled 'dry' outside the bottle stands completely vertical with the wooden crutch fitting snugly under Long John's armpit and dowelled into the body just above the left knee. The base of the crutch and the under surface of the right shoe are the only two components which keep the figure in an upright position, so it is vital that they are well glued down. To make doubly sure of this some green Plasticine from the background can be pressed round these areas when the figure is in the bottle. The hair and beard were made from saffron coloured Sylko laid on the glued surface a few strands at a time. A thin strip of white linen 1/8 in wide was glued round the wrists to represent the white cuffs sported by gentleman of this period. The thin black leather for the hat was cut out as shown and the brim given a thin coat of glue, which was pressed into an upright position when tacky and then placed on the head at a suitable jaunty angle. Should the neck of the bottle be rather narrow it is advisable to fit the parrot on the figure's shoulder before the hat is added.

Chapter 13

The old gas-lamp cleaner

This is an instance of a model not being planned beforehand but rather of a subject being chosen to fit a bottle. The bottle in the illustration was brought from Cornwall by a friend and I would estimate its age somewhere in the region of 80-100 years. It looks very much like one of the old 'cough-mixture' bottles [an elixir much loved by the Victorians. This type of bottle often carried a grandiose label extolling the contents at great length and apparently the range of complaints that these mixtures cured was immense, irrespective of whether they were drunk or used externally as a liniment! These odd potions often contained hair-raising ingredients such as laudanum, opium and various strengths of chlorodyne to which alcohol was added, making a mixture which would make a shire horse wilt. Such concoctions were often administered to small children as a form of 'knock-out drops', so that the parents of the typically large families of those days could spend Saturday night in the local gin-palace in an atmosphere of comparative peace!] An old and fascinating bottle in any event but the question was how to utilise it to the best advantage? Obviously it was not suited to a highly detailed ship model because of the flaws in the glass, which are inevitable in bottles of this type and era.

One evening I happened to be reading one of those excellent reproduction newspapers depicting old street scenes, when I came across just the subject and shape to fit the bottle in question. It was an old gas-lamp cleaner, ideal for making and fitting into the old tinted bottle, which measures $7^5/8$ in $\times$ $2^3/8$ in $\times$ $1^1/2$ in, tapering to $1^1/4$ in. I can vividly remember as a small boy one of these stalwarts (affectionately known as 'Old Lampy') dressed in an old jacket, corduroy trousers tied below the knee with a bootlace, armed with a bucket, window leather, spare gas-mantles and pockets bulging with various spanners, pipe grips, etc. He would be puffing away on a clay pipe full of 'twist' tobacco, which gave off such ghastly aromas that people would ask whether he was smoking dead mice! This was, of course, in the 'bad old days' when one man had to do about four jobs to provide for his family. Old Lampy would mount his ladder, give the glass panes a wipe over and do any necessary repairs, such as the replacing of broken gas-mantles.

So, having a theme for a model the first question was what medium to use for the basis of the model, for it had to be easily mouldable and preferably black. Bitumen, as used by folk in the electrical trade for protection of underground cables, was just the thing. It's a good workable medium when warm and never sets rock hard in normal temperatures but it *is* inflammable. The bottle in question has a neck length of 3 in so the whole of the model is actually enclosed in a space of $4^5/8$ in $\times$ $2^3/8$ in $\times$ $1^1/2$ in (or slightly less in fact because of the thick glass). The actual cost of the material was less than 50 pence, so this should not make any appreciable dent in even the most modest bank balance.

The base of the gas-lamp is an old toothpaste tube cap; the upright stem made from the wooden dowel part of an old dishmop; the two 'arms' are two round 1 in nails and the 'glass' for the four panes of the lamp are made from a rigid transparent lid of a chocolate box. The top of the lamp is made from a single shape cut from a plain postcard and the bucket formed from thin sheet lead, (although tin or a piece of postcard would serve just as well). The handle of the bucket is an ordinary dress-makers pin, with the head and point cut off and bent into a semi-circle, with just the last $1/32$ in curled upwards at each end. The figure of the man is carved entirely in beech, as are the two sides of the ladder; the 13 rungs of the ladder being made from Chinese toothpicks. Careful measurements (as with all models in bottles) are essential and as one can see from the illustration and the diagrams, the foot of the ladder fits snugly into the bitumen base, whilst the top rests with each side on an arm of the lamp, just underneath the lamp proper.

A start is made on the lamp by tapering one end of the the wooden dishmop handle (which is just ordinary $3/8$ in dowel) down to $5/16$ in. Only a 3 in length of this is needed, but it is easier to handle in the long length and then cut it to the right size afterwards. Cut ten grooves length-wise along the dowel with a fine saw and a three-cornered file. Then drill a $3/32$ in hole in the top at the $5/16$ in end to a depth of $3/8$ in and another hole horizontally $3/8$ in from the top to accommodate the two 1 in round nails. Then drill out the toothpaste cap to $3/8$ in to receive the base of the gas-lamp stem. The next component to be made is the square base of the lamp proper, to hold the four panes that form the lamp. This base was made from a $1/2$ in square of hardwood $3/32$ in thick, with four grooves in a square being cut out with a sharp scalpel. These grooves, which must be angled slightly outwards, hold the base of the four panes. A hole is drilled in the centre of the square to receive a $1/2$ in woodscrew which must not be more than $3/32$ in wide. Countersink the screw hole and test the square base with the screw into the top of the gas-lamp stem and run the screw in and out a few times with a small radio screwdriver to ensure an easy fit, remembering that this has to be screwed into place *inside* the bottle later on. The four 'glass' panes were cut with a fine saw and finished off with a file, the four being held together to get them to a uniform size of $5/8$ in $\times$ $1/2$ in $\times$ $5/16$ in. The sides of these panes must be filed to an angle of 45° to ensure a good fit. As previously mentioned, the top of the lamp itself is cut in one piece from a postcard and scored with the *back* of a knife to facilitate folding where indicated. All the gas-lamp components can now be painted in dark green Humbrol gloss. Paint the edges of the panes with bands $1/16$ in wide to simulate the lamp frame. This can be achieved neatly by masking the centre of the each pane with a piece of Sellotape which is peeled off immediately after painting. All these components can now be left to dry completely whilst the next components are made.

The sides of the ladder are made from two lengths of beech, or other hardwood $3^3/8$ in long $\times$ $3/16$ in wide $\times$ $1/16$ in thick. Round off the two sides at each end and drill 13 equidistant holes with a $1/16$ in drill. To do this accurately hold the two sides firmly together whilst drilling. The 13 rungs, made from Chinese toothpicks, require rounding off at each end and then place them in *one*

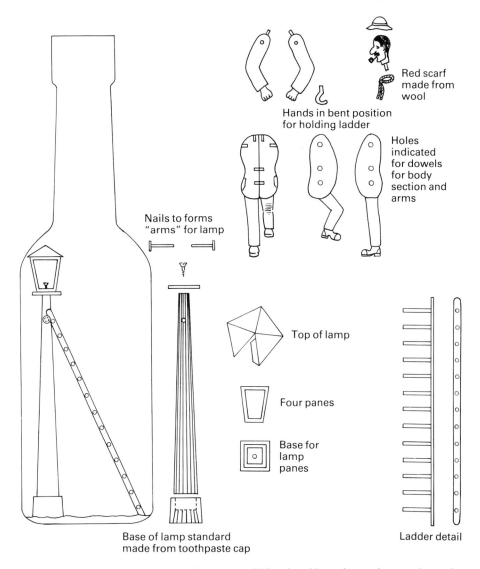

Hands in bent position for holding ladder

Red scarf made from wool

Holes indicated for dowels for body section and arms

Nails to forms "arms" for lamp

Top of lamp

Four panes

Base for lamp panes

Base of lamp standard made from toothpaste cap

Ladder detail

Fig 35: *A slightly more advanced figure model like the old gas-lamp cleaner obviously requires more time and patience.*

side of the ladder to test for bottle neck clearance, (which in my case was ½ in wide, the same length as the rungs, so a slight rub down with fine glasspaper was all that was necessary to allow for the slight enlargement in size once it had been painted). Then all 13 rungs can be glued into *one* side of the ladder. (A file mark should be made in the bottom of the ladder sides for it is easy to get them the wrong way up and then the rung holes will not match up.) The ladder can be painted white or black or a plain polyurethane varnish can be used instead.

The figure of the lamp cleaner is carved with saw, scalpel, file and glasspaper respectively. As one can see from the drawing the body is in two halves longitudinally, one leg and one side of the body in each piece. The two sides are not identical however, as the left leg is in the bent position and is on the rung above the right, as if the figure is climbing the ladder. The two pieces of beech used for the trunk and leg pieces measured $1^3/4$ in $\times$ $^1/2$ in $\times$ $^1/4$ in each. The two sections were positioned and joined with two $^1/16$ in dowels. The arms were cut from beech $^3/16$ in $\times$ $^1/2$ in $\times$ $1^1/8$ in and shaped in the slightly bent position, so that the hands, carved in a natural bent position would be gripping the sides of the ladder in a climbing position. The arms were dowelled $^1/8$ in from the top of the shoulders, the dowels being fitted to the arm pieces and the $^1/16$ holes to receive these being drilled to a depth of $^3/16$ in at the shoulders. When the dowels are fitted, test the position of the arms in relation to ladder and if neccesary recess them into the shoulder slightly. Drill two vertical $^1/16$ in holes down into each trunk section at the neck, into which the head/neck dowels will fit and which will help lock the two trunk sections together. The jacket on the figure is indicated with scalpel cuts at lapel, pocket and hem. Then paint the 'jacket' with Humbrol matt black and the shoes too. The trousers can be painted matt brown to represent the corduroy cloth which was standard working wear in this era.

The head and neck can be carved from one piece of $^3/16$ in dowel. As stated in Chapter 12 carving heads and features is not the fearsome task it may seem and with a little practice on a piece of scrap wood a reasonable likeness can be achieved quite easily. Flesh coloured Humbrol paint is used for the face and hands, with a slight touch of red on the nose (as these lamp-cleaning men were not noted for being abstemious!) Black matt paint can be used for the hair and eyebrows can be indicated by two short wisps of black cotton and a bushy 'beer-strainer' moustache added if desired, using thin black wool. Eyes can be made to look quite realistic if a tiny dab of white paint is put into a drilled eye socket with the point of a pin and when it's dry a tiny dab of blue paint can be put in the centre of the white. A few inches of wool, (which I filched from my wife's work basket), red is ideal, was made into an ideal neckerchief (as wages for this paticular job in the Victorian era did not run to collars and ties, except perhaps for weddings). Drill two $^1/16$ in holes vertically in the neck and fit dowels into these to coincide with the holes already drilled in the two trunk sections. The bucket can be made of thin sheet lead, or thin card will do just as well. If you use card cut a strip 1 in $\times$ $^5/16$ in and roll this round the tapered end of a pen, cut it to size and glue, trimming the top and the bottom when dry. An elastic band will hold the card in its proper shape until the glue dries. Paint silver (or cover with silver paper) and pierce holes in the top to accommodate the handle, made as described previously from a bent pin. It is not necessary to put a bottom in the bucket as it will be embedded in the bitumen at the foot of the ladder, so put a tiny circle of silver paper to indicate the water level about three-quarters the way up the sides. When the paint is perfectly dry on all the components the assembly can begin.

Warm the bitumen in the palm of your hand and fashion it into small sausage shapes and drop these on to the bottle base. Only a $^1/16$ in depth is necessary so spread the bitumen with a long steel rod until a reasonably flat surface is achieved. Glue the stem of the lamp-post into the toothpaste cap and, when this is dry, place it towards the 'back' of the bottle about $^1/2$ in from the side, to allow for the width of the top of the lamp which is $^1/2$ in square when assembled. Tilt the stem of the lamp towards the centre of the bottle and lower the square wood base with the screw *in situ*, using the split bamboo gadget. With a long

The old gas-lamp cleaner in a Victorian 'cough mixture' bottle.

radio-type screwdriver screw the lamp base firmly to the top of the lamp stem, ensuring that it is square with the back of the bottle. Next insert the 'glass' panes. The first pane will need glue only on the bottom edge but the others will require glue on one side as well. Add one by one to form the square and press them together for a time until the glue sets hard. Then fold the top of the lamp and insert it into the bottle, having first coated the tops of the panes and the overlapping tab on the lamp top with glue. Fix this firmly in position. After moving the lamp standard back into the vertical position leave it for at least 12 hours to dry out thoroughly. The fact that the lamp standard is moveable need cause the modeller no concern, for it is later fastened securely when the ladder is assembled, the bottom of which is embedded in the bitumen, whilst the top is glued to the gas-lamp arms.

The side of the ladder with the attached 13 rungs can now be placed in the bottle, which has to be laid at this stage in assembly. It is as well to embed this first side in a tiny blob of Plasticine fixed to the side of the bottle as a temporary holding measure whilst the remaining side of the ladder is eased into place. Afterwards the Plasticine can be removed but do not rush, give the ladder plenty of time to dry. Righten the bottle.

It is now a simple matter to place the ladder in position with a length of $^1/_{16}$ in wire bent $^3/_{16}$ in from the end. Press the bottom of the ladder into the bitumen base and lean the top of the ladder on to the arms of the lamp. Apply spots of glue at these points and leave to dry.

Lay the bottle on its side again and insert one half of the figure, apply a thin coat of glue, insert the opposite half and press the sides firmly together ensuring a perfect joint. When the figure is dry, put the bottle in the upright position again and, with the bent wire, position the figure on the ladder with the face on a level with the panes of the lamp. The left foot in my model is on the eighth rung and the right foot on the seventh. A dab of glue is all that is necessary on the shoe soles for the time being as the arms will be added next and will, with the curvature of the hands round the sides of the ladder, make the whole a firm fixture.

Fix the arms next using the split bamboo gadget with a dab of glue on the dowels before they are pressed firmly into position. Then add small dabs of glue to where the hands rest on the ladder. Leave for a while to dry. Now the head and neck part can be inserted and the woollen neckerchief in position adds a good finishing touch, besides effectively hiding the neck joint.

The figure in the model illustrated is sporting a briar pipe, easily made from a piece of bent wire or carved from wood, painted brown, or if a clay pipe, white. In this case you will have to drill a hole in the mouth at an appropriate angle with a $^1/_{16}$ in drill and $^1/_8$ in deep. The only remaining component to add is the bucket, which should be positioned at the base of the ladder. Allow about a week to dry out before sealing the bottle with cork and sealing wax.

Chapter 14

King Neptune and the mermaid

Here is another suggestion for a figure model which is rather unusual in that it depicts an underwater scene. A Johnny Walker 40 oz whisky bottle measuring $11^5/8$ in $\times$ $3^1/4$ in square was chosen for this particular model. The bottle is cleaned in the same way as described in Chapter 2 and when perfectly dry two sides and the base are painted on the inside. Plenty of time must elapse for the paint—which in this case is an ice-blue shade—to dry and, if possible, two coats are preferable. The best way to do this is to paint one side at a time, laying the bottle flat afterwards to ensure an even surface. Then repeat for the other side and when these are perfectly dry, the base of the bottle can be painted. Repeat for the second coat.

From the illustration one can see that the model includes a 'shipwreck' which is, in this case, the bows of a coastal schooner. The accompanying diagrams shows how this bow section can be formed from laminations of beech, mahogany or some other hardwood. It is very important that these strips or laminations are completely *flat* so that they lie perfectly level in 'layers' one above the other. Careful sanding is necessary on the 12 flat pieces and also on the thick top section. The stem post of the ship, to which all the strips are glued, is made of the same material, the section cut as shown. The modeller will appreciate that the diameter of the bottle neck determines the width of the strips, or strakes, which do not lie flat to the bottle side, but are 'bedded' in a wad of Plasticine. This Plasticine acts as padding to give the bows of the ship a three dimensional curved look and also holds the wreck firm to the back of the bottle. So, when all the strakes have been cut to shape and you are satisfied that they are a snug fit in the stem, the curved (convex) edges and the stem should be given one or two coats of Humbrol matt black paint. A $^3/16$ in hole should then be drilled, as indicated on the diagram, in the thicker topmost section and deeply countersunk on the inside. This is the hawse hole through which the anchor cable (chain) comes. A length of fairly fine chain is used for the cable (the chains from one of those old wooden Swiss clocks are ideal for this) a 6 in length is ample and the end is pinned into the inside of the thick (countersunk) section and a good blob of adhesive will fix it firmly. Test this during construction to ensure that it passes through the bottle neck without damage to chain or paint. The other end of the chain is attached to the anchor, or rather that part of the anchor which shows above the sea bed, ie, the stock and shank.

The anchor stock is made from a piece of hardwood $^1/8$ in square tapered towards each end, while the shank of the anchor is a round iron nail, with the head and point filed off. The nail should then be flattened slightly at one end—a section of $1/8$ in is sufficient—and drilled with a hole wide enough to accommodate the width of a split link of the chain; then the wooden stock is drilled in the centre with a drill of the same diameter as the shank. Insert the shank to within $1/16$ in of the drilled end and the split end link of the chain is neatly clinched closed, a dab of glue ensures that this stays fastened. Give both chain and anchor a coat of matt black paint.

My figures of 'Neptune' and the 'mermaid' were carved entirely in beech, but mahogany would be equally suitable, but avoid softwoods for this or *any* bottle model as these bruise too easily. The heads were carved from $1/4$ in beech dowel and the bodies from $5/8$ in square section. The arms were made from beech $1/4$ in thick. It is a good idea to vary the angles of the elbow joints as this looks more natural. The legs were made from the same material and again the joints were made at different angles. The feet and hands were carved separately and dowelled with $1/16$ in dowels, glued and carefully sanded to hide the join. Do not make the angles of the arms too acute or they will not pass through the bottle neck. The hands being small and delicate, especially those of the Mermaid, must be carved very carefully. They can either be made in the flat or bent position, but the essential part of the carving is to make four *fine* cuts first to form the fingers and thumb, remembering that the latter, first and little finger must be correspondingly shorter. (A small fine saw blade and fine file are essential for this job.) When you are satisfied with the carving (try some on a piece of scrap wood first, if you prefer it) drill $1/16$ in holes in the wrist parts and correspondingly in the arms, joining these with a $1/16$ in dowel and glue. These should be sanded down when dry to hide the joints as much as possible.

Carve two heads (see fisherman in bottle, Chapter 12) one feminine and one masculine-looking. The hair for both figures was formed from strands of Sylko laid on a thin coat of adhesive a few at a time. Grey was used for Neptune and gold/yellow for the mermaid. Carving the mermaid's tail is rather a delicate job and a card template should be made to ensure the curve is not too pronounced to prevent it from going through the bottle neck. The tail was painted a greenish-blue and jointed to the body afterwards with a $1/16$ in dowel and glued. The fin end of the tail was also made separately, dowelled and glued in the same way.

The shark, which goes into the bottle in one piece, was also carved in beech, the fins being formed from $1/16$ in strip and fitted into recesses in the body. As sharks have high pointed tails, this component must be constantly tested for bottle neck clearance, (always remembering the slight difference a coat or two of paint can make to a wooden carving). The upper part of the body is painted in dark grey while the underside is white. A book from the library on sea creatures will be a great help in getting the shape and colouring of the shark correct and there are also some excellent illustrations of other marine creatures you may wish to incorporate in the model as a background embellishments. The eyes and teeth of shark can be also emphasized by using celluloid or sheet ivory and the mouth of the shark can be made to look rather more menacing if a line of red paint is carefully applied to represent his 'bloody' gums. (For narrow lines such as this I find it more convenient to apply paint with pointed end of a cocktail stick.) A $1/16$ in hole is drilled in the belly of the shark to accommodate a dowel that projects from a wooden base which, in due course, is placed in position in the bottle. This is to hold the shark in a natural swimming position

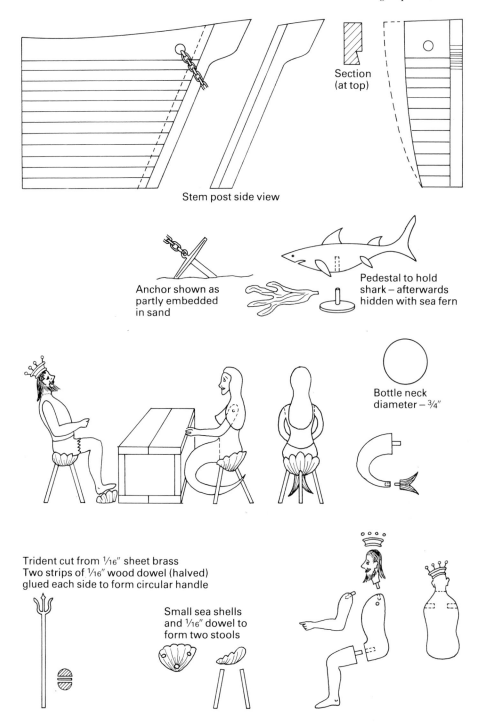

Section
(at top)

Stem post side view

Anchor shown as
partly embedded
in sand

Pedestal to hold
shark – afterwards
hidden with sea fern

Bottle neck
diameter – ³⁄₄″

Trident cut from ¹⁄₁₆″ sheet brass
Two strips of ¹⁄₁₆″ wood dowel (halved)
glued each side to form circular handle

Small sea shells
and ¹⁄₁₆″ dowel to
form two stools

Fig 36: *The various components needed for the Neptune and mermaid model.*

and the dowel can be covered after insertion by a fragment of sea-fern, (which you can obtain either from the seaside or from any shop which stocks aquarium accessories). Add a layer of fine sand to the sea bottom to fill in the gaps between any of the other existing areas.

The hull of the shipwreck is first to be placed in the bottle. Insert the stem post of the ship with a liberal coat of glue on the side that will adhere to the side of the bottle, making sure that you allow enough room for the length of the strakes, the topmost being the longest. Allow two or three days to dry. Make a piece of Plasticine to the required measurements of the wreck, roll up and insert into the bottle. Press firmly into place. Commence with the bottom (smallest) strake and embed this in a liberal coat of glue both at the stem groove side and the underside of the strake, leaving ample time to dry out. The strakes are then added one at a time to build up the hull and the more time you allow at each stage of this operation the better. Check constantly for the alignment of the hull. Extra care must be taken when putting on the top bulwark section of the bows as the anchor cable (chain) is attached to this. Leave the anchor and chain resting on the bottom of the bottle for the time being. On completing the hull it is a good idea to add strands of sea fern at both ends of the hull as this not only adds a distinctly overgrown wreck-effect but the added adhesive gives extra hold to the hull. As soon all is dry spread a thin coating of glue on the 'sea bed' round the wreck and sprinkle in some fine dry sand. The best way to do this is to fill a thin glass tube with sand and trickle it into the bottle. The excess can be shaken out immediately afterwards.

The figure of the shark can be placed in next, resting on the base with its pro-truding dowel. When this is firmly glued down, the base is covered with sand as before and the part of the dowel which is visible is masked by a wisp of sea fern. The anchor cable/chain and the anchor can also be glued down at this point and in its turn surrounded by sand.

The stools on which the two figures sit are relatively simple to make, the seats being made from small pink scallop sea shells. Select two—a fairly large one for Neptune and a smaller one for the mermaid but make sure that they are small enough to go through the bottle neck and of a good depth to accommodate the seated figures. Drill the shells as shown in the drawing at about $1/16$ in from the edges and at an angle to allow the legs of the stool to splay out slightly for stability. The stool legs are made from $1/16$ in dowels tapered at the ends to ensure a good fit into the seat and the floor. Assemble these without glue to see that they stand level. Assemble the figures of Neptune and the mermaid to see how far apart they are eventually going to be. This is most important because the wooden sea-chest has to fit between the figures and the measurement must be correct to $1/16$ in.

The chest, see in the diagrams, is made of beech or mahogany strips $1/8$ in thick and $9/16$ in wide. The top and bottom of the chest are both formed from two strips of wood, with two pieces of masking tape (as used in the motor trade for paint spray protection) cut to $1 1/8$ in $\times 3/4$ in and fixed in position as indicated in the diagram. Although the masking tape is self-adhesive it is advisable to use a thin smear of glue on as well, as an added precaution. When the glue is dry, fold the two sections together and test for bottle neck clearance, leaving a little undersize to allow for layers of paint. The two side pieces of the chest are also joined with masking tape hinges to the ends, so that when in the open position they look like letter L's (ie, are at 90° to each other). Holes are drilled for two

$^1/_{16}$ in dowels which ensure that the two L-shaped sides fit perfectly together. These four pieces should also be tested for bottle neck clearance. The chest was placed in position before the figures so it could then act as a temporary 'workbench' on which to make up the figures ready for glueing and dowelling

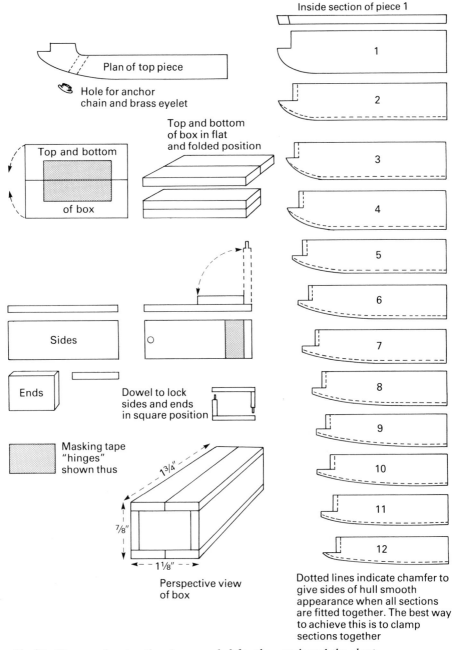

Inside section of piece 1

Plan of top piece

Hole for anchor
chain and brass eyelet

Top and bottom
of box in flat
and folded position

Top and bottom

of box

Sides

Ends

Dowel to lock
sides and ends
in square position

Masking tape
"hinges"
shown thus

$1^3/_4$"

$^7/_8$"

$1^1/_8$"

Perspective view
of box

Dotted lines indicate chamfer to
give sides of hull smooth
appearance when all sections
are fitted together. The best way
to achieve this is to clamp
sections together

Fig 37: *Diagram showing the pieces needed for the wreck and the chest.*

An unusual underwater scene of Neptune and a mermaid.

together. Careful measurement is essential in the positioning of the chest so sufficient room is left for Neptune's feet and for the mermaid's tail. At this stage it does help to mark the positions of all objects on a card template of the internal dimensions of the bottle to ensure that the two figures sit as near as possible to the chest. When you have finally checked the positions of all components, put the hinged chest bottom through the bottle neck and glue down firmly, masking tape hinge uppermost. Then put in one of the L-shaped hinged sides with a thin coat of glue on the edges to join on to the chest base, repeated for the opposite side. Unite the two dowels in their holes and adjust before the glue dries to ensure that all angles are at 90° and that all sides are flush with the base of the chest. When completely dry, coat the top edges with glue and then put the chest top in position, tape side down. Correct alignment and leave to dry out thoroughly.

The two stools can now be assembled by placing the shells convex side up on top of the chest and glueing the three dowels in place. Leave for a little while to dry. Afterwards put a good blob of glue on the base of the stool legs and place them in their respective places. These must be left for a long time to set as both Neptune and the mermaid have to be well glued into the hollow of the shells and *must*, of course, be absolutely immovable whilst the arms, legs, heads and tail are added. The mermaid's tail is adjusted so that the tail section fits snugly between the stool legs. Assembling the figures may seem a lengthy business with all the time needed to allow one component to dry out before adding another, but it is one of those cases where 'it is quicker to be slow'. A further coating of sand can be done now, around the seated figures and the chest, also fill in any patches that may have been missed.

The model is now nearing completion so any other embellishments you may care to add, such as a miniature bottle of rum, playing cards, etc, can now be glued on to the top of the chest. Small dried sea ferns can be glued in position round the chest as this enhances the appearance of this 'underwater' model, as well as helping to cover up any joints in the chest you may not be happy about! If you wish to add a further touch of realism to the model, a few brightly coloured fish—easily carved from a $1/16$ in strip of wood—can be glued to the back of the bottle. A realistic 'eel' can be made from plastic-covered single-core electric cable, in grey or black, bent into undulating curves and then glued securely to the sea bed. Remove any glue and paint smears from the inside of the bottle and allow at least 14 days for the contents of the bottle to dry out completely. Then a suitable cork is glued into the bottle neck and, if desired, a Turk's Head knot can be added as an extra embellishment. This model will be a source of wonder to your friends with its 'three-D' effect and with careful handling will last forever.

Chapter 15

Self portrait—an unusual miniature

This very small figure model was constructed in 1979 and upon its completion, several friends remarked that the figure bore a close resemblance to myself, so it was given the above title. It is a quite a tiny model and was understandably a trifle difficult to make, but well worth the effort. It was exhibited in France that same year, after which a replica was given to La Musée Naval et Municipal at Fort Balaguier, La Seine sur Mer, France.

The bottle used for this model is a miniature Haig dimple which measures $3^3/4$ in $\times 1^1/4$ in $\times 1^1/4$ in with a bottle neck diameter of $^{15}/32$ in. The table was made from two lengths of $^1/16$ in beech strip $1^1/4$ in $\times ^5/16$ in, hinged with a piece of masking tape. The table legs were made from four lengths of $^1/16$ in dowel, $^5/8$ in long overall, $^1/16$ in being fitted into the table top. The stool was also made of $^1/16$ in strip and is $^7/16$ in square, the corners being rounded off with a fine file. The four stool legs were $^1/16$ in dowel and $^3/8$ in long, $^1/16$ in being allowed for fitting into the top. The legs fitted into the four holes which were drilled at an angle to allow them to be splayed out like the legs on a milkmaid's stool. The stool was small enough to enter the bottle already glued together.

The head and body were made from a piece of carved boxwood, which was hard to get but is ideal for miniature work. This piece measured $1^1/8$ in long by $^1/4$ in square, the last $^1/4$ in allowed for the head, for which the width was reduced to $^3/16$ in before carving. The face and head were painted in flesh-coloured Humbrol paint, as were the hands, described later. The body, legs and arms were painted in matt dark blue, with the exception of the the shirt front, which was white, to which was added a tie made from grey thread. The legs of the figure were made from blue plastic covered single core electric cable 1 in long and $^3/32$ in diameter with $^1/8$ in of wire bared at each end. Two copper wire ends were given a liberal blob of solder which was later filed into the shape of shoes and painted gloss black. The other end fitted into two holes in the trunk of the body as shown in the diagram. The arms were fashioned from $^1/16$ in dowel and to form the joint in the elbow, a 90° V was cut, almost right through, given a dab of glue and held until set in a right-angle position. This kind of joint can be made by making a miniature 'clamp' of pins driven into a piece of flat wood. To make sure the dowel does not break, it is a help to dampen it first. The shoulder ends of the dowel were rounded off and the $^3/32$ in left at the other end was filed into the shape of hands. The shoulder ends were drilled with a very fine drill and later fitted into the shoulder part of the trunk with two $^1/2$ in brass

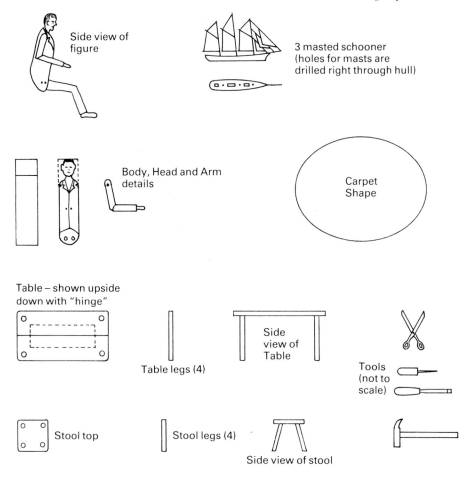

Fig 38: *Diagram showing the parts required of a miniature self portrait model.*

pins, cut down to $^1/_8$ in long. Particular care must be taken when drilling the shoulder holes in the dowel.

The carpet, the first item to go in the bottle, was a piece of coloured linen, cut into an oval shape $1^3/_4$ in $\times 1^1/_4$ in, rolled up like a cigarette and pressed on to a coat of adhesive spread on the base of the bottle. Allow plenty of time for this to stick and put a few tiny objects on top to ensure thorough adhesion. Also allow plenty of drying out time as this is a very small bottle and the carpet will eventually have to have the stool, table etc, resting on it.

The small three-masted schooner on the table is exactly 1 in long, the hull length $^7/_8$ in and the bowsprit, which protrudes at the bows $^1/_8$ in, has to have the same length stuck into the hull. The hull of this tiny ship was also carved from boxwood and sanded very carefully to shape, so the finest glasspaper is necessary. At this small scale, rigging of any kind was not attempted and the masts, bowsprit and yards were made of fine iron wire and painted a stone colour. The hull was painted black but this was only a personal choice, it could be red or green. The height of the masts were; foremast and mizzen $^1/_2$ in, mainmast $^5/_8$ in and the upper and lower yards (gaffs) were $4/64$ in and $5/64$ in long respectively. Three holes were drilled into the hull to accommodate the masts and one in the bows for the bowsprit. The sails were made from ordinary bond paper and glued to the masts and yards. Each mast complete with sails and yards was put in the bottle starting aft then forrard, mizzen, main and fore. Test the holes in the hull first in case they are not free of paint. They should be a good push-in fit, not too tight, but tight enough to be in line with the fore and aft run of the ship and at 90°. The three deck-houses were made from thick white card which, of course, needs no painting. Deck-house tops can either be left white or painted in grey or green. The jib and forestay sails are put in place by dabbing with adhesive at the head and foot of the sails, the top adhering to the foremast, the foot to the bowsprit. Leave this tiny ship to dry for a while during which time small tools can be made which, in the model, lie on the table giving the illusion of work being done on the ship.

The chisel has a handle made from a piece of $1/16$ in dowel, $3/16$ in long, which was bored with a drill fine enough to take a $1/2$ in long brass office pin, flattened on the blade part and filed to an edge. The chisel and handle measure $7/16$ in overall. The bradawl handle, also made from a $1/16$ in dowel, was bored out to take a similar pin, but left with its pointed end. The handle is $1/8$ in long and the overall measurement is $1/4$ in. The hammer was made from a $1/8$ in nail to form the head, which was cut down to $5/16$ in long, after filing to resemble a claw hammer (the claw part being formed by cutting a groove with a fine saw $1/16$ in deep, the inside of the claw being rounded with a fine round file). The hammer head was then drilled for the shaft and a $1/16$ in dowel was inserted into this. The dowel was shaped to resemble a hammer shaft with a fine file and glasspaper. The overall length of the hammer is $5/8$ in. The scissors, which measure $5/16$ in $\times$ $1/4$ in, were made from 40 gauge iron wire, the loops of the handles formed

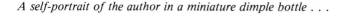

A self-portrait of the author in a miniature dimple bottle . . .

And a younger version, this time in a 1-litre dimple bottle.

by wrapping the wire round a fine darning needle. Then file the overlapping wire off flush. The rest of the wire which formed the blades was heated and hammered flat, cut to an angle at the ends and the cutting edges sharpened. The blades were then drilled with a $^{13}/_{1,000}$ in drill and a very tiny brass pin used as a rivet, which was cut down almost level and tapped flat. The scissors are quite difficult to make but if the modeller is skilled at small work they present no problem. These scissors do actually *cut*, but like the rest of the tools they were glued afterwards to the table top, within easy reach of the figure who is depicted as working on this very tiny ship.

A tapered cork was then prepared whilst the contents of the bottle were drying out. This was drilled lengthwise to within $^1/_8$ in of the narrow end, then a hole was drilled horizontally across this with a $^1/_{16}$ in drill. Two $^1/_{16}$ in dowels were cut to $^1/_4$ in lengths and the ends which fitted into the cork at the narrow end were cut at 45°. A little adhesive was put on these and by inserting a pointed cocktail stick down the vertical hole in the cork the two wooden pegs were moved outwards so that they projected wider than the bottle neck. After thoroughly drying out for some days, the bottle neck was sealed and a Turk's Head knot added (the knot being painted red) and the completed model then looked quite neat and typically 'impossible'.

Chapter 16

The two domino players

In this example there are two figures in a tinted 2-litre bottle, seated facing each other across a table, engrossed in what looks like a serious game of dominoes. There is a full set of 28 of these, each domino measuring $\frac{1}{9}$ in $\times$ $\frac{2}{9}$ in $\times$ $\frac{1}{16}$ in. These need not all have the appropriate 'spots' on as only about half will have their 'faces' showing. As most people know how to play dominoes, the choice of pieces can be left to the modeller, but it is customary to put down the largest, ie, the double-six first, followed by six-five, double-five, five-four, and so on. Therefore, these higher ones would probably be the ones to make. The question of how to indicate the dots on the dominoes was a bit of a poser, for to make these tiny dots with a paint brush would be as easy as striking a damp match on a tablet of soap! So, the problem was solved by coating the $\frac{1}{16}$ in metal strips with Humbrol black matt paint, then, once dry, scoring the dividing line found across the middle of dominoes with a sharp scalpel. Naturally this took off the paint and the silver metal line underneath showed up admirably. The dots were then drilled with a $\frac{1}{32}$ in drill and also showed up very well. This operation of course, needs some very careful work and it is advisable to mark the position of the dots first with a sharp needle, to act as a guide for the drill.

Apart from the metal strip used for the dominoes and the sheet ivory (or white celluloid) used for the eyes and teeth of the figures, the rest of the material used was beech. The arms and legs were made from $\frac{1}{2}$ in beech dowel and the body sections made from $\frac{5}{8}$ in section (square) wood, as were the two carved heads, hands and boots. The table, which measures 2 in $\times$ $2\frac{1}{2}$ in was made up of three pieces of beech each $\frac{11}{16}$ in $\times$ $\frac{1}{16}$ in which were hinged on the underneath side with masking tape, to enable it to pass through the bottle neck in the form of a triangle. The table legs were $1\frac{7}{8}$ in long overall and made from $\frac{1}{4}$ in dowel. These were turned with an electric drill, using a sharp scalpel and fine glasspaper. The last $\frac{1}{16}$ in of both ends of each leg is reduced to $\frac{1}{16}$ in diameter to enable them to dowel securely in both table top and floor.

The three-legged stool was also made of $\frac{11}{16}$ in $\times$ $\frac{1}{16}$ in beech strip, but as the top has a diameter of $1\frac{1}{4}$ in it needed only two strips hinged with the masking tape like the table. The stool legs were made from $\frac{1}{16}$ in dowel, 1 in long overall, with $\frac{1}{16}$ in at each end secured in the top of the stool and the floor. One of the figures is seated on this stool while his partner is seated on a beer crate, which is 1 in $\times$ $\frac{1}{2}$ in $\times$ $\frac{5}{8}$ in. This is also made from beech strip but the six internal compartments are made from three pieces of card; again a plain postcard is ideal. The card is cut to shape as shown in the diagram and slit

A model of two domino players involved in a serious game.

halfway so that the sections fit together, thus these must be cut accurately.

The floor was made in four sections of $^{11}/_{16}$ in × $^{1}/_{16}$ in strip and measures 5 in × $2^{3}/_{4}$ in overall, being supported by two 'joists' ($2^{3}/_{4}$ in × $^{7}/_{8}$ in × $^{1}/_{2}$ in) carved on the underside to fit the inside curve of the bottle. To ascertain the inside curvature of the bottle, thin cardboard templates must be made. The simplest way to do this is to stand the bottle on its end on the card and mark the outside curve with a pencil. A guess at the thickness of the glass (say $^{3}/_{32}$ in) will enable you to draw a parallel curved line to match the outside circumference. This should give the approximate shape for the underside of the 'joists' that support the floor. The floorboards were marked with a 6H pencil to indicate 5 'planks' on each $^{11}/_{16}$ in strip and given a coat of polyurethane varnish.

The various sections which go to make up the figures, stool, table, floor, beer crate etc, are fully indicated in the diagrams, but, of course, if this model is placed in a bottle of different shape or size, these various components must be modified to suit. I found that the appearance of the figures was enhanced by making the angle of the knees different for no two people sit at a table in exactly the same position, so I portrayed one figure with his feet further back. The table in this model does in fact overlap the knees of the two players by approximately $^{1}/_{4}$ in and the space between the toecaps of the boots of the partners is just 1 in. The table top, when fitted, should clear the height of the knees by about $^{1}/_{8}$ in.

It is important that a drawing should be made of the floor, (a portion of which is shown in the diagram) to mark the position of the three-legged stool, the legs of which fit into holes in the floor, as well as the four holes for the table legs. The beer crate was not dowelled into the floor, but merely glued down as the base of this crate provides sufficient surface for adhesion. The heads in this model are shown with entirely different facial expressions, so that it looks as if one player is losing. This is quite easily done by just reversing the curvature of the mouth!

The shade of hair can be left to the personal choice of the modeller and black, brown, grey or white Humbrol paint is ideal for this purpose. The body sections marked 'Left' and 'Right' on the diagram are cut to size and rounded at the edges, so that when the two halves are put together they assume the shape of a body, with the waistline shown by recessing slightly with a file and glasspaper.

The diagonal lines shown on the drawings are cut $^{1}/_{8}$ in deep and are slots to 'inset' the arms so that they look more natural and with the dowels provide extra support for the arms. The arms are round in section and rounded off at the shoulders. The arms are held in the correct position in the slots in the body section and drilled for the dowels so that these are located exactly. The upper arm dowels, at the shoulders, are then fitted. It is not necessary to make these any longer than ¼ in as these are for positioning only. The joints at the elbows are cut at 45°, matched up at the same angle with the upper arms and the dowels similarly fitted. The arms are also drilled at the wrists, where they will be dowel-jointed with the hands. The hands of one player were carved in the clenched position, whilst the others were almost flat. The table top, legs and stool were painted in gloss brown and the crate and boots of the two players in black. The 'suit' of one of the players was painted in Humbrol matt grey and the other in matt dark blue. The jacket lapels on the figures can be easily shown by means of thread damped and coated with glue and tapped into the body after painting by means of tiny pins. The thread is well pressed down with the blade of a radio screwdriver and when dry the pins are removed and painted over with a thin coat of the appropriate shade. This makes the lapels stand out well but must, of course, be done fairly quickly before the glue has a chance to dry. Buttons on jackets can also be added, which is quite easy to do; just cut off the heads of some fairly large pins and drill holes in the appropriate positions, apply a dab of glue and press the pins in. These can be left in their natural bright state or painted to suit jackets.

Leave all these components to dry and whilst this is being done the floorboards can be marked and then given a coat of polyurethane varnish, keeping the *sides* of each clear to ensure a good fit. Should any varnish run on to the sides, sand it off on a flat surface. The holes for the stool and table must be drilled when these two components are assembled. The two back legs of the stool fitted in holes drilled ³/₁₆ in from the back edge of the floor, and the front leg of the stool was of course dead centre in the width of the floor. Make the stool top complete with masking tape and fit legs, but do not glue yet — this will give position for the holes. The same procedure is followed for the table. Number floorboards underneath L1, L2, R3, R4 to ensure that they will be in the correct order when they are inserted. The beer crate was positioned at the extreme edge of the floor, exactly in the centre, with the compartment side facing the bottle neck. Test each part of the figures constantly with dowels in position for bottle neck clearance, allowing for paint thickness, of course.

The strip of linen 5 in × 2¾ in, which forms the base, should be cut with sharp scissors to avoid fraying and glued in position ¼ in from the end of the bottle, using the seam of the glass is an alignment guide. When the linen strip has completely dried out, insert the back joist followed by the front and, working quickly, these should be aligned by pressing at either end with a stout steel rod. These must be dead level and alignment can be checked by looking through the bottle neck. The floorboards were drilled and fitted with pointed ¹/₁₆ in dowels as in the board meeting model (see Chapter 17) and tested in the joists for position prior to insertion. All joints, dowels etc, should be kept free of paint. Test assemble the figures for position in the bottle and mark the position of the boots on the floor with a pencil outline, or, if preferred, cut an outline shape and glue it to floor (use *thin* card only). Glue down the boots of figure nearest the base end of bottle first and leave to dry. Then insert the stool top into the bottle in its folded position and turning it upside down glue on the three legs. Use the split bamboo gadget for this. After allowing plenty of time to dry, upturn the stool and glue the legs into the holes in the floor. Let these dry. Then place the appropriate lower leg of the back figure into position in the furthest boot, followed by the other lower leg, then the thigh parts. Follow

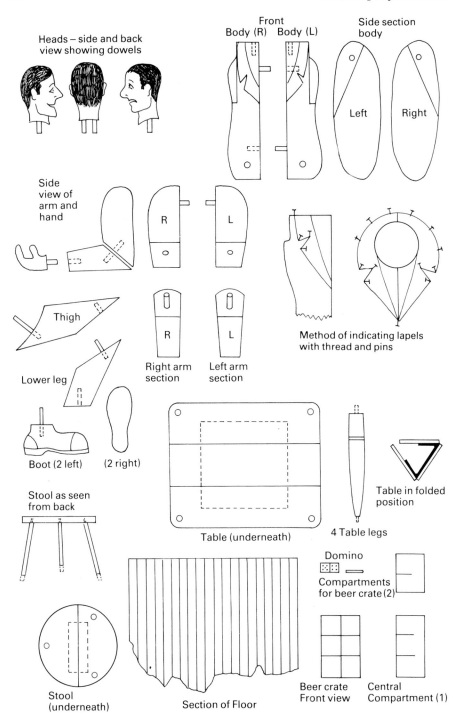

Fig 39: *Diagram for the two Domino players. Remember to vary the angle of arms and legs, as well as the expression on the faces.*

Fig 40: *Plans for the construction of a stand.*

Two end sections 4½″ × 1⅛″ × ⅝″

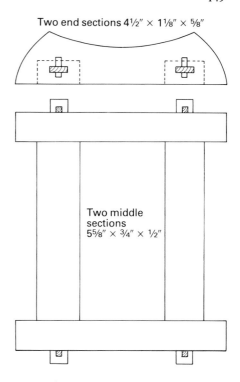

Two middle sections 5⅝″ × ¾″ × ½″

fairly quickly, before the glue has chance to set, with the two body sections and the head, which, with the two dowels in the neck, 'lock' the body sections together. Do not attach arms yet. A generous blob of glue on the posterior of the figure will make him hold firm to the stool. Leave for a good period to dry out.

Fold the table top into a triangle and insert into the bottle, opening it out upside down. Insert table legs into the ¹/₁₆ in holes drilled in each corner and after leaving time to set, up-turn the table and ease the legs into the floor, pressing down well. Put a few weights, such as small coins, or nuts to keep the table top flat until dry. Then add the arms of the back figure beginning with the shoulder joints, followed by lower arms and hands. It is not a difficult matter to balance two dominoes on their edges in each hand, with a spot of glue on the edges. Place the remainder of your 'spotted' dominoes face up on the table positioned as if a game were in progress. The remainder of the dominoes, the 'undotted' ones, can be stuck to the table face down.

The boots of the other figure can be stuck down and the sequence of adding limbs repeated. The beer crate was placed in the bottle next, glued down and left to dry, having been eased under the posterior of the figure. Allow the model to dry out for at least a week and then glue the cork in firmly.

The choice of stand is left to the modeller, but as this is a fairly large bottle, a good deep curve should be used to keep the bottle firm and secure. It can be made in beech, mahogany or oak, either stained or with the wood left in its natural state and then varnished with polyurethane. This is an ideal type of varnish for bottle modellers as it is thin, dries quickly and with two coats gives a good hard mirror finish.

Chapter 17

The board meeting—a more advanced model

This model depicts a board meeting of an imaginary shipping company in the mid-19th century, the eight people concerned discussing the merits of a new clipper ship. The whole model, which is composed of over 300 components is enclosed in a 2-litre green-tinted Spanish wine bottle, which measures 14 in × 4^1/8 in with an internal bottle neck diameter of ^{13}/16 in (just about the same size of an old farthing). There are eight men inside the bottle, seven of whom are seated round an impossibly large-looking table, being addressed by the eighth figure, a rather dignified chairman in black morning coat and grey trousers. The heads and bodies of the figures are carved from ^{1}/4 in beech dowel, the faces all differing slightly in shape and expression. Each head was shaped by saw, scalpel, file, dentist's 'burrs' and a small drill. Carving the head and face of each model entailed about two hours work. They have brown, white or grey hair and some also have beards. All are sporting white shirt fronts and bow ties or cravats. Again I stress that the main thing to remember when embarking upon models of this type is that *every* article or component must be made exactly to size and completed before *anything* is inserted in the bottle. No matter how great the temptation might be to start on the model, and the many delays might seem frustrating at first, this is the best and only way to save a whole lot of headaches later on. Also, as with the simpler models described earlier, every component must be tested for fitting at the various stages.

Three joists are necessary to support the floor owing to the weight which will later be placed on it (see the Domino Players, Chapter 16 on how to obtain the right curve for the joists to fit correctly inside the bottle.) The floorboards are made from strips of beech ^{11}/16 in × 7 in × ^{1}/16 in, with five 'planks' scored on each with a 6H pencil or an extra-fine black ballpoint pen. Give each board a coat or two of polyurethane varnish. The seven chairs have seats made of ^{1}/16 in strips of beech, the dimensions of which are given in the accompanying diagrams. Care must be taken when drilling the ^{1}/16 in holes at the four corners of each chair seat for these accommodate the dowels which form the chair legs, while the central hole has a dowel of the same diameter but projecting ^{1}/8 in *above* the top surface of the chair. This small projecting dowel is to 'anchor' each seated figure absolutely rigid in his chair. The reason for this immovability will be appreciated later on when the modeller has to add the arms and legs on each figure.

As previously stated, the figures have bodies carved in beech, drilled where shown with a ^{3}/32 in drill to receive the heads, arms and legs. The arms and legs

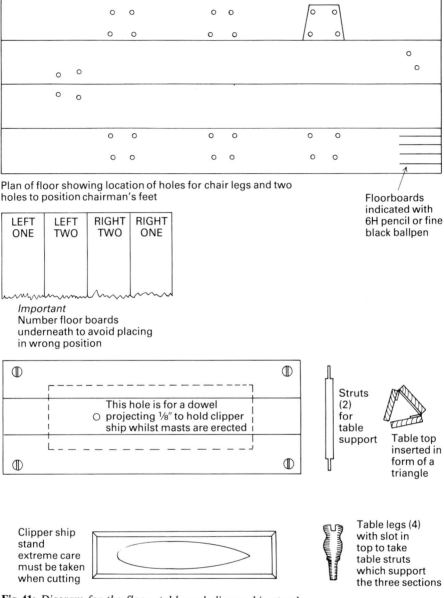

Plan of floor showing location of holes for chair legs and two
holes to position chairman's feet

Floorboards
indicated with
6H pencil or fine
black ballpen

LEFT ONE	LEFT TWO	RIGHT TWO	RIGHT ONE

Important
Number floor boards
underneath to avoid placing
in wrong position

This hole is for a dowel
O projecting ⅛" to hold clipper
ship whilst masts are erected

Struts
(2)
for
table
support

Table top
inserted in
form of a
triangle

Clipper ship
stand
extreme care
must be taken
when cutting

Table legs (4)
with slot in
top to take
table struts
which support
the three sections

Fig 41: *Diagram for the floor, table and clipper ship stand.*

were made from three-core and seven-core plastic covered electric cable,
respectively, (the ideal medium for this purpose, as it can be bent or adjusted
slightly when the figures are *in situ*.) The ends of the three- and seven-core cable
must be bared ³/₁₆ in at one end and the strands twisted tightly together, for this
end will later fit into the shoulder of the figures. The other ends of the three-
core cable are bared for ⅛ in and twisted lightly together to form a base for the
hands which can be made from Polyfilla or, preferably, solder. I used the latter

and found 'Baker's Fluid' the most suitable, as copper wire has an affinity for solder, so applying a small blob of solder with a small electric soldering iron was a simple job. Use a fine file to shape the hands. The $1/4$ in ends of the seven-core were slightly splayed out and covered with solder to form the shoes. To avoid using too much heat at this point, which will melt the plastic covering, wrap a little damp thread at the point where the bared wire protrudes from the plastic. The arms must be bent in the folded position, so that the lower arms will rest on the table but allow sufficient room for the model ship which will occupy the table centre. The legs must be placed so that the feet do not get in the way of the feet of the figure sitting opposite.

The method of carving the heads is the same as described for the simpler models. Flesh coloured Humbrol paint was used for the faces with a touch of red for the noses and cheeks of the less abstemious, whilst matt brown, grey and black was used for hair and beards. White paint or teased-out cotton wool was used for the hair of the senior members. Ties and cravats were fashioned from coloured thread, flattened out with a steel rule and tied round the necks in a bow with fine tweezers. The necks were cut off at $3/16$ in long and inserted in the appropriate holes previously drilled in the body parts. These were not affixed all facing forwards but looking in different directions as if engaged in conversation.

Two small pictures were cut from a furniture catalogue and were rather appropriate for they depict sailing ships and thereby add a touch of authenticity to the model. The clock on the mantelpiece was an old, lady's wrist-watch which would just pass through the bottle neck after the strap loops had been filed off. Try and get as small a watch as possible, but *not* a chromium or stainless steel one. Chromium plating did not come on the scene until the 1930s, so this would look extremely odd in a model depicting the mid 1800s. Take the back off the watch and remove as many of the 'works' as you can, (if possible, all of them) to keep the weight down. The 'clock', as it now is, fits in a wooden surround but not glued, as case and clock enter the bottle separately and will later be placed on the mantelpiece when *in situ*. The clock case or surround was made from two strips of beech $1/16$ in $\times$ $1\frac{1}{8}$ in $\times$ $1/2$ in and the horizontal part of the stand measures $1\frac{1}{8}$ in $\times$ $3/4$ in $\times$ $1/4$ in. The respective pieces and the method of assembly are shown in the diagram.

The white and gilt fireplace, (shown upside down in the diagram to indicate the method of construction more clearly) is also made from $1/16$ in beech strip. It is hinged with masking tape to keep all the relevant components together for insertion in the bottle neck, the ornamental strip acting as a support to keep the upright parts vertical. (The uprights are shown shaded in the diagram.) The notches at the bottom of the uprights are to fit in the gap left between the floor boards and the bottle base. The curved section at the back of the mantelpiece and at the backs of the uprights are to fit the convex base of the bottle. (Make a card template first to achieve the correct curvatures.) The fireplace surround is gloss white paint and 'gilt'.

The four table legs were made from $1/4$ in dowel which was turned in an electric drill with the aid of a woodcarver's small chisel, a fine file and glasspaper. These beech legs are $7/8$ in long and are inset into the floorboards to a depth of $1/16$ in, a slot being cut into the tops to give support to the table and two $1/8$ in strips of beech are cut to fit into these slots. The diagram will indicate the method of inserting these. The table is $4\frac{7}{8}$ in $\times$ $1\frac{3}{4}$ in and made of $1/16$ in

A view of the board meeting model showing much of the detail (Sheffield Newspapers Limited, Sheffield).

thick beech strips. In the diagram the underneath view shows the position of the table legs and the dotted lines show the position of a linen or masking tape hinge which enables the table top to be put in the bottle in the form of a triangle.

There is only one standing figure in this model, that of the dignified and bespectacled chairman who is wearing a morning coat made of thin linen, painted matt black, with grey trousers (which were actually represented with matt grey Humbrol paint.) This figure goes into the bottle complete, except for the arms. As previously mentioned the legs are formed from seven-core wire, the shoes being blobs of solder filed down to the appropriate shape. In this instance, however, just *one* strand of wire was left straight and unsoldered on each foot to anchor the standing figure to the floor. He has one arm slightly bent at his side while the other is bent to rest on the table with a miniature 'prospectus' in his hand. This prospectus measures $5/8$ in $\times$ $1/2$ in with nine lines of printing on it, which was, in fact, a facsimile of some document photographically reduced in a furniture catalogue. This came in perfectly for the model, for no matter how good a person may be with a mapping pen, the typography is so minuscule as to be virtually impossible to reproduce by hand.

On the table is a black-edged stand on which rests a clipper ship, fully rigged with 26 sails. The stand is made from $1/16$ in beech strip and is 3 in $\times$ $3/4$ in. Great care must be exercised when cutting out the shape for the underneath of the ships' hull.

Some idea may be gleaned of the intricacy of this ship model when one realises that the overall size is only 3 in $\times$ $13/4$ in, the latter being the height of the mainmast. Other relevant measurements are given on the diagram.

Plasticine was spread thinly on the stand to give a wave and wake effect, the colours used being dark blue and white. The method of making this ship is exactly as described in the earlier pages of the book, but naturally the measurements have to be scaled down.

After cleaning the bottle, a strip of black linen measuring 7 in × 3¼ in is coated on one side with a slow-drying latex-based adhesive, rolled up and inserted in the bottle. Move it quickly into place and position it ⅜ in from the end of the bottle, making *quite certain* that the strip of linen is equidistant at each side of the seam in the bottle. It is *most important* that this strip of linen is stuck down firmly. If in any doubt lift the edges with a bent wire and put on more adhesive for added security, as it must be borne in mind that this strip of linen is the 'foundation' on which the floor supports, floor, table, chairs etc, all rest. So, after repeatedly pressing this down to ensure a close adhesion, allow to dry for at least two days in a warm, not hot, place.

Next, having cut the three floor supports to the exact inside shape of the bottle, lay the floorboards on them and drill holes ³⁄₃₂ in diameter and ¼ in deep. A pointed dowel should be inserted, glued into the planks, but not into the supports, and cut off flush on the upper side. Repeat for all boards. Afterwards the seven lots of four holes are drilled for the chairs (1⅝ in from the ends and ⅛ in from the edge), four holes for the table legs and two holes to accommodate the wires in the feet of the chairman. Next, coat the curved undersides of the three floor supports with a slow-drying adhesive and place these in the bottle; the one nearest the base of the bottle is put in first. Ensure that these are flush with the edges of the black linen, the middle support being equidistant between the end two. Then look through the bottle neck and ascertain that these are uniformly level. This is *important* otherwise the floorboards will not bed down correctly and these should be easy to adjust with a stout wire before the adhesive sets. Check again for alignment and allow to dry for at least two days so that any condensation disappears. Then lay the floorboards. I found it a help to number these on the underside (as indicated in the diagram), otherwise they can get in the wrong order. Glue the planks down and tap the pointed dowels down with a small weight, such as an ordinary nut fixed to the end of a thick wire. Leave to dry and, if at all possible, leave a series of small weights on it, such as half-penny pieces, to maintain a steady pressure on the floor until the adhesive has set. The next item to be put into the bottle is the fire-place surround; this being first coated with glue on the concave edges and at the two cut-out slots, which of course butt on to the back edges of the floor. Ensure, by looking through the bottle neck, that the horizontal mantelpiece is absolutely central in the width of the bottle and it is advisable to stand the bottle on its base, whilst checking that the two vertical supports are properly in position. Then allow the adhesive to set, with the fireplace a secure fit to the base of the bottle. Next, roll up the glossy card which forms the fire back, having bent the two tabs (A) at right angles and scored the fold (B) so that this can be glued to the floor whilst tabs (A) are glued inside the fireplace. There will be a slight gap between the fire back and the end of the bottle. This space will hold the fire itself which can be effectually simulated by using some gold foil from the cap of a champagne

Right. Fig 42: *The components for this complicated model are many, but as always it is vital to check continually for bottle neck clearance.*

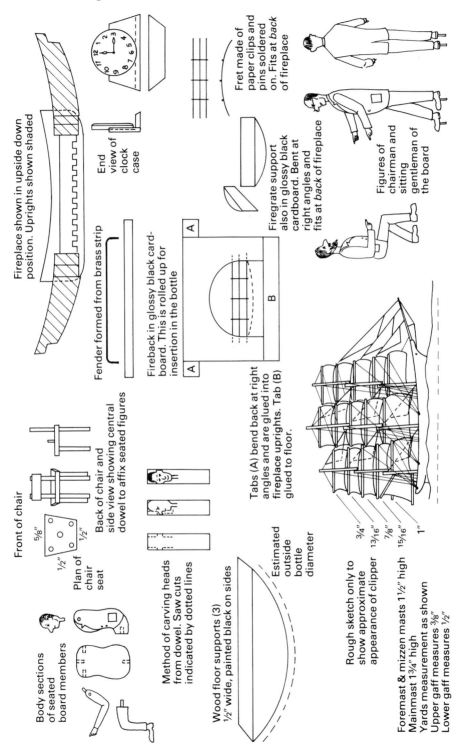

Fireplace shown in upside down position. Uprights shown shaded

End view of clock case

Fender formed from brass strip

Fret made of paper clips and pins soldered on. Fits at *back* of fireplace

Figures of chairman and sitting gentleman of the board

Firegrate support also in glossy black cardboard. Bent at right angles and fits at *back* of fireplace

Fireback in glossy black cardboard. This is rolled up for insertion in the bottle

Tabs (A) bend back at right angles and are glued into fireplace uprights. Tab (B) glued to floor.

Front of chair

Back of chair and side view showing central dowel to affix seated figures

Plan of chair seat

Body sections of seated board members

Method of carving heads from dowel. Saw cuts indicated by dotted lines

Wood floor supports (3) ½" wide, painted black on sides

Estimated outside bottle diameter

Rough sketch only to show approximate appearance of clipper

Foremast & mizzen masts 1½" high
Mainmast 1¾" high
Yards measurement as shown
Upper gaff measures ⅜"
Lower gaff measures ½"

¾"
13/16"
⅞"
15/16"
1"

bottle, (affluent friends are an asset here!) painted black at the bottom or, better still, small fragments of coal interspersed with tiny dabs of red paint. If you opt for real coal this must be added after the gold foil is *in situ*.

The steel fret, as shown in the diagram, is now bent into a curved section, the two ends glued and carefully inserted into the fire-place. The easiest way to do this is to coat the glossy card first with the glue, using a long wire bent into a semi-circle at one end. The steel fret rests on the fire-grate support. The lacquered brass fender is also added at this stage as well as the two pictures, (or one large one), but ensure that they are high enough up not to be obscured by the clock case, which is the next item to be added.

The shape of the clock case shown is only a suggestion and obviously can be altered, providing it can pass through the bottle neck. Put a sizeable blob of glue at the back of the watch and convey this to the case on the mantelpiece on the end of a length of $1/8$ in wire or split bamboo cane, which is eased gently in. As soon as it is in position, stand the bottle upright for at least 24 hours. Some people may find the insertion of small objects into bottles rather difficult—a steady hand is a great asset and the split bamboo cane is a useful gadget for these jobs (a diagram of this gadget appears in Chapter 12).

Now it is time to start moving in the furniture! Start off with the chair which backs on to the mantelpiece. Get the chair on its side next to the four holes into which it will eventually fit and put a small dab of glue at the foot of each chair leg, then lift the chair upright and ease into the holes. It helps if $1/16$ in is marked off with a hard pencil at the foot of the chair legs, as an indication as to whether they are level. I also marked each chair underneath with a number, so that each one was sure to fit in the correct position; I also marked the posterior of each figure, so that each one was matched to his own chair where he sat—uncomfortable but secure—on the projecting central dowel. (The chairs can be marked on a paper plan beforehand so that, after testing for fit, the modeller can place them in their respective positions with a minimum of difficulty.) Glue all the chairs in as securely as possible, leave to dry and then place in the first figure, which is, of course, the gentleman with his back to the fire. The other six seated figures (or to be more correct, the heads and trunks) are then placed in the bottle, working from the back of the bottle forward, pressing each figure firmly into his respective chair. Leave these once again to thoroughly set, as these must be absolutely firm fixtures when the legs are affixed, which is the next job. Again working from the back of the bottle forward, commence fixing the legs which must *not* be crossed for this will affect the level of the table. However one figure could have his legs apart while the figure opposite can have his together, or perhaps one bent back at each side of the chair, in this way the arrangement of the seated figures shown in slightly different postures avoids that 'wooden' look. After getting all the pairs of legs in place apply a small amount of glue to the sole of each shoe but do *not* add the arms yet, as the table is next to be assembled. Insert the table legs and check that none of the knees of the figures are higher than the table legs. As was done earlier with the chair legs, it is a great help to mark off $1/16$ in on the table legs with a pencil, to make sure that the table top will be completely level. Then affix the two table struts or supports and check that the four legs are completely vertical before leaving to dry out. The table top is then folded into its triangular shape and gently eased into the bottle. Leave folded whilst you apply a coating of glue to the tops of the table legs and the supporting struts. The table top can now be opened out and placed into position, checking carefully for alignment. Put a series of weights on the table top—a number of small coins can be used—to press the table top completely flat. Give this about 24 hours to dry out.

When you are satisfied all the components are completely dry, the arms of the figures can be added, again working 'aft to forrard' (as a seaman would put it). The arms can be bent into different positions. In the model illustrated the end figure has one arm raised as if making a point to the Chairman but the other six figures *must* have arms close to their bodies to leave room for the model ship on its base.

The model of the clipper ship is made in the same way as described earlier in the book (see Chapter 6) but is, of course, on a correspondingly smaller scale; a simpler model, such as a two-masted schooner (see Chapter 3) could be substituted. To ensure that this model is secure whilst erecting masts, deck fittings etc, a short dowel (indicated in the diagram) is fitted through the table top into a hole in the hull of the model ship. When making the smaller version of the clipper ship it is important to remember to leave the rigging threads much longer as you are working in a much longer bottle. When everything appears to be absolutely dry put a little ordinary table salt in a roll of paper and insert it into the bottle neck as an extra safeguard. This will absorb any excess moisture which might not be apparent and will prevent any condensation problems later on. Then any glue marks can be removed from the bottle with a wad of damp cotton wool but great care must be taken to avoid knocking any of the figures. Paint smears can be removed in the same way, substituting Humbrol thinners.

Another view of the same model (David Muscroft).

The figure of the Chairman with his prospectus is the last component to go into the bottle, minus his arms and spectacles. Be sure to apply quite a good quantity of glue to both the projecting wires and the soles of his shoes as well as to his right hand, which rests on the table, for these three glueing points are his 'sole means of support' as it were. When his position is finally fixed the prospectus can be glued on the table at the side of his hand. If you have not been fortunate in finding one of these miniature reproductions, a tiny wine bottle and glass will do instead and any friend or schoolboy who has access to a chemistry lab can make these quite easily from small-bore glass tubing. The spectacles, which were purposely placed rather near the end of the Chairman's nose, were easily made from a short length of copper fuse wire, the round eye pieces being formed by winding the wire round a thin iron nail and just tipped with a small soldering iron to fuse it into one firm component. Then, when all the paint and glue marks have been removed, a good tight cork is put in the bottle neck, lightly coated with glue and pressed well in.

If one desires, the cork can be recessed ($^1/_{16}$ in) and a Victorian farthing, polished and lacquered, can be glued on top of the cork. An ornamental Turk's Head knot will add the finishing touches to this rather difficult and complicated model. However, I am sure the modeller will agree that it is entirely different from the usual bottle models and despite the rather prolonged construction time, it will be visible evidence of time well spent as well as being something of an achievement. I would regard this as one of the most intricate models I have ever made, and it has aroused world-wide interest, having been shown at exhibitions as far apart as America and Japan, as well as at many major shows in the UK.

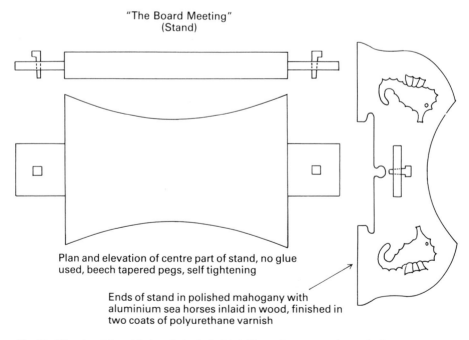

"The Board Meeting"
(Stand)

Plan and elevation of centre part of stand, no glue
used, beech tapered pegs, self tightening

Ends of stand in polished mahogany with
aluminium sea horses inlaid in wood, finished in
two coats of polyurethane varnish

Fig 43: *The stand for this bottle included inlaid sea horses on the end pieces.*

List of materials
Small drill from $\frac{1}{16}$ in to $\frac{1}{8}$ in
Several water-colour paint brushes
Suitable 2 litre bottle
Humbrol paints in matt brown, blue, grey, gloss white, black brown and red
Humbrol thinners
3 ft of beech or other hardwood strip, $\frac{1}{16}$ in thick $\times$ $\frac{11}{16}$ in wide
2 ft of $\frac{1}{4}$ in dowel
Silko or other quality cotton, white, black and brown
1 ft of $\frac{1}{2}$ in square beech
$1\frac{1}{2}$ ft of $\frac{3}{4}$ in beech, for figures
1 ft of three-core cable
1 ft of seven-core cable
Blue/green and white Plasticine
Small ladies' watch
Strip of gold ribbon, (often found on chocolate boxes) for fireplace ornamentation and sleeves of the sea captains' coats
Small electric soldering iron
Baker's fluid solder
Paper clips and tiny ($\frac{1}{2}$ in) office pins
Cotton wool (white)
Chinese toothpicks for yards on model ship
$\frac{1}{16}$ in dowel or cocktail sticks for masts, etc
A few sheets of good bond paper for sails
Some good seasoned beech or mahogany for the stand, 12 in $\times$ 6 in $\times$ $\frac{1}{2}$ in
6 in square of $\frac{1}{16}$ in aluminium for sea-horse ornamentation on stand
6 in square of black, glossy card
Gold foil, from champagne bottle
Bamboo garden cane 15 in $\times$ $\frac{1}{4}$ in
Three or four 15 in long wires $\frac{1}{16}$ in, $\frac{1}{8}$ in and $\frac{1}{4}$ in
Small pictures and typescript facsimiles from catalogues or magazines.

Appendix 1

A short glossary of nautical terms

Abaft Towards the stern of the ship.
Aft Towards the stern of the ship.
Athwartships Fitments at 90° from the fore and aft line of the ship, between stem and stern, ie, the seats in a dinghy or rowing boat are arthwartships and in nautical phraseology are called thwarts.
Backstays Rigging leading from royal, topgallant or topmast down to the bulwarks abaft the shroud.
Barque A vessel of three, four or five masts. All masts are square-rigged except the aftermast.
Barquentine A vessel of three to six masts. Only the foremast is square-rigged.
Belaying pin Heavy, handled metal pins for belaying running rigging in pin rails or fife rails.
Binnacle The stand on which the ship's compass is fitted. Usually made of wood with brass (non-ferrous metals) fittings, as iron or steel would deflect the needle.
Block A wooden or metal shell which contained sheaves (pulleys).
Bolt rope Heavy rope with which sails are edged to strengthen them.
Bows The front of a ship.
Bowsprit The heavy boom projecting from the bows to which foremast stays and jib stays are secured.
Braces The rope (later wire) leads from the ends of the yards, which led to the sides of the deck to brace or move the yards.
Brails Ropes which horizontally hauled spanker sails to the mast.
Brig A vessel with two masts, square-rigged on both masts.
Brigantine A vessel with two masts. The foremast is square-rigged and the main

mast fore-and-aft rigged.
Bulwarks The sides of a ship's hull which extend from poop deck to fo'c'sle deck.
Bunt The middle of a square sail.
Buntline The ropes leading from the foot of square sails which were led through blocks via yards and mast to the deck. Used to haul up sail preparatory to stowing.
Capstan The main capstan of a ship was on the fo'c'sle deck. Could either be turned by means of capstan bars or, in later days of sail, these were steam-powered from a donkey boiler. Many of the big barques would have four capstans on the main deck for raising yards or heaving braces. A system of pawls or ratchets prevented these slipping backwards.
Clewlines Ropes attached to the bottom corners of square sails.
Clews The lower corners of square sails, also lower after corners of fore and aft sails.
Cradles Supports on which ship's boats rested when hoisted inboard.
Crojacks The lowest sail on the mizzen mast of a three-masted ship or four-masted barque.
Davits A means of hoisting and lowering ship's boats
Deadeyes Wooden blocks with three eyes, grooved round edges, spliced to shrouds and backstays, the lower ones to the chain plates on the sides of the hull. A lanyard was rove through these and the rigging was thus kept taut.
Dolphin Striker (or *Martingale*) A wood (later metal) projection beneath the

bowsprit which was rigged with stays to counteract the upward pull of the jib and topmast stays.

Doublings The overlapping parts of built-up masts.

Driver The gaffsail on the after mast of a ship or barque, and also the fifth mast on the seven-masted schooner *Thomas W. Lawson.*

Ear ring The outer corners in the head of a square sail. The rope by which the corner is fastened to the yardarm.

Fall The running end or moving parts of a tackle.

Fife rail A rail at the foot of a mast to which running rigging was led and secured by belaying pins.

Fore The opposite of aft, as in forepart, forepeak, foremast, etc.

Forecastle Abbreviated to fo'c'sle—a relic of the sailing warship days when ships had fighting 'castles'—the after one being an aftercastle, where long bow and cross bow archers were stationed in battle. The fore part of a ship.

Forepeak Compartment at bow of a ship beneath top deck, in which paint, oil, kerosene, coiled hawsers, rope etc, are kept.

Freeboard The height of a ship's bulwarks above the sea.

Furling Securing the sail to its yard by means of gaskets.

Gaffs The spars of a fore and aft sail.

Gaff topsail The fore and aft sail abaft the topmast.

Gaskets Thin ropes to fasten a sail to the yard when furled.

Grommet A circle of rope.

Guys Rope stays from a boom to the sides of a ship.

Halyards Ropes which are used to hoist yards and gaffs, also flags.

Head stays Stays from foremast to bowsprit.

Heel The bottom or foot of a mast.

Hoops Rings of wood which enable a gaffsail to be hoisted up the mast.

Jackstay The rail on top of yards to which sails were rove through. Also a handrail for the crew when furling or unfurling sails.

Jib A staysail on a head stay.

Jigger The aftermost mast in a four-master.

Lifts Ropes which supported the yards from the masts.

Lower mast The bottom section of a mast.

Luff The forward edge of a fore-and-aft sail.

Mainmast The mast abaft the foremast.

Martingale The more correct term for the Dolphin Striker.

Mizzen mast The mast abaft the mainmast.

Parrels Wooden rollers to allow a yard to be hoisted or lowered on a mast.

Pawls The ratchet devices fitted to a capstan to prevent run-back.

Pin rail A rail inside the bulwarks to accommodate belaying pins.

Plimsoll Line Statutory load line instigated by Samuel Plimsoll as a guard against illegal overloading of ships. Many marks such as F denote fresh water line, WNA denotes Winter North Atlantic, etc. Ships are lower in the water off the mouth of a large river (eg, Amazon) and higher in a strong salt content. Many owners in the early days of sailing merchant ships were not very fussy about loading for *they* didn't have to sail in their ships and there were a few cases of the Plimsoll Line being obliterated and painted a foot or so higher. They reasoned that a ship with, say, a cargo of wood couldn't sink!

Poop The after deck of a ship.

Rake The fore-and-aft slope of masts from the vertical.

Ratlines Ropes (clove hitched) across the shrouds on which the crew climbed aloft.

Red Duster Merchant Navy flag consisting of three-quarter area of red with Union Jack at top nearest flagpole head.

Reefs Ropes attached to both sides of a sail to reduce area presented to the wind.

Reeve To put ropes through blocks to form a purchase.

Rigging screws Used in the latter days of sail. These incorporated a right- and left-hand thread to tension rigging.

Royal The top square sail on a mast carrying six sails.

Royal mast The mast above the top gallant. In later days was one spar.

Running rigging Rigging used in operating sails. Applies to braces, buntlines, clewlines, or any rigging involving blocks or purchases.

Scuppers The outside edges of the decks which, with the bulwark holes, drained away sea water.

Sheave A grooved pulley inside a block.

Sheerline The curve of a ship's hull from bow to stern.

Ship A three-, four- or five-masted vessel, square rigged on *all* masts.

Shrouds Heavy rigging of rope or wire which supported masts, led to deadeyes or rigging screws on ship's side.

Standing rigging Rigging which supports masts and yards.

Stays Ropes or wire which support masts in fore-and-aft direction or athwart ships.

Staysails A triangular sail set on fore-and-aft stays.

Stern The back or rear of a ship.

Studding sails Often abbreviated to 'stun'sails'. Narrow sails run out at the sides of the square sails in clipper days.

Stun'sails Short for studding sails.

Tackle A system of blocks and ropes to form a purchase for lifting gear.

Thwarts 'Seats' in a ship's boat.

Thwartships Across the ship.

Topgallant mast The mast above the top mast.

Top mast The mast above the lower mast.

Topping lift A rope which led from the boom of a gaffsail, through the block at the mast head, down to the deck to hold the boom when furling sail.

Truck The top of the mast.

Unbend To cast off the sails from the yards.

Windlass Horizontal winding winch (as opposed to a capstan which is vertically mounted) on fo'c'sle and used for hoisting the anchor.

Yard The spar which carries a square sail.

Yardarm The extreme ends of the yards.

Appendix 2

Conversion table of inches into millimetres

Inches		0	1	2	3	4	5	6	7	8	9	10	11
0	mm	0.00	25.40	50.80	76.20	101.6	127.0	152.4	177.8	203.2	228.6	254.0	279.4
$1/16$	mm	1.59	26.99	52.39	77.79	103.1	128.6	154.0	179.4	204.8	230.2	255.6	281.0
$1/8$	mm	3.18	28.57	53.97	79.37	104.8	130.2	155.6	181.0	206.4	231.8	257.2	282.6
$3/16$	mm	4.76	30.16	55.56	80.96	106.4	131.8	157.2	182.6	208.0	233.4	258.8	284.2
$1/4$	mm	6.35	31.75	57.15	82.55	108.0	133.4	158.8	184.2	209.6	235.0	260.4	285.7
$5/16$	mm	7.94	33.34	58.74	84.14	109.5	134.9	160.3	185.7	211.1	236.5	261.9	287.3
$3/8$	mm	9.53	34.92	60.32	85.72	111.1	136.5	161.9	187.3	212.7	238.1	263.5	288.9
$7/16$	mm	11.11	36.51	60.91	87.31	112.7	138.1	163.5	188.9	214.3	239.7	265.1	290.5
$1/2$	mm	12.70	38.10	63.50	88.90	114.3	139.7	165.1	190.5	215.9	241.3	266.7	292.1
$9/16$	mm	14.29	39.69	65.09	90.49	115.9	141.3	166.7	192.1	217.5	242.9	268.3	293.7
$5/8$	mm	15.88	41.27	66.67	92.07	117.5	142.9	168.3	193.7	219.1	244.5	269.9	295.3
$11/16$	mm	17.46	42.86	68.26	93.66	119.1	144.5	169.9	195.3	220.7	246.1	271.5	296.9
$3/4$	mm	19.05	44.45	69.85	95.25	120.7	146.1	171.5	196.9	222.3	247.7	273.1	298.6
$13/16$	mm	20.64	46.04	71.44	96.84	122.2	147.6	173.0	198.0	223.8	249.2	274.6	300.0
$7/8$	mm	22.23	47.62	73.02	98.42	123.8	149.2	174.6	200.1	225.4	250.8	276.2	301.6
$15/16$	mm	23.81	49.21	74.61	100.0	125.4	150.8	176.2	201.6	227.0	252.2	277.8	303.1

Appendix 3

A list of reference books

Some of the following books are now out of print, but the majority are still available. Those out of print should be available in good reference libraries.

Coastwise Sail, by John Anderson (Percival Marshall).

Strange Sea Road, by Warren Beadnall (Jonathan Cape).

West Country Sail, by Michael Bouquet (Journal of Commerce).

The Four Masted Barque, by Edward Bowness (Percival Marshall).

The Cutty Sark, by Frank G. G. Carr (on sale abroad).

The Twilight of Sailing Ships, by Robert Carse (Harrap).

The Clipper Ship Era, by Captain A. H. Clark (Patrick Stephens).

The Wheel's Kick and the Wind's Song, and *Windjammers of the Horn,* by Captain A. G. Course (Sea Breezes).

The Tall Ships Pass (Herzogin Cecilie), by W. L. A. Derby (Jonathan Cape), since reprinted by David and Charles.

The Duchess (Herzogin Cecilie), by Pamela Eriksson (Secker and Warburg).

How to Make Clipper Ship Models, by E. H. Hobbs (Brown, Son and Ferguson).

Voyaging, by Captain J. W. Holmes.

Ghosts on the Sealine, by A. A. Hurst (Cassell).

The Great Age of Sail, edited by Joseph Jobé (Patrick Stephens).

The Cape Horn Breed, and *All Hands Aloft,* by Captain W. H. S. Jones (Jarrolds).

Mother Sea, and *Pully Haul,* by Elis Karlsson (Oxford University Press).

The China Clippers, The Colonial Clippers, The Down Easter, and the *Log of the Cutty Sark,* by Basil Lubbock (Brown, Son and Ferguson).

The Last of the Windjammers, Vols I and II, by Basil Lubbock (A. H. Stockwell).

Some Famous Sailing Ships and their Builder, Donald McKay, by Richard McKay (Patrick Stephens).

Down Easter Captain, by Captain W. J. Moore, DSC RD (A. H. Stockwell).

The Last Grain Race, by Eric Newby.

The Last of a Glorious Era, by Ronald Pearse (Conway Maritime Press).

Men and Ships Around Cape Horn, by Jean Randier (Arthur Baker).

The Voyage of the Cap Pilar, by Adrian Seligman.

The Last Sail Down East, by Giles M. S. Tod (Barre Publishers, Barre, Mass, USA).

Masting and Rigging the Clipper Ship and Ocean Carrier, Sailing Ship Rigs and Rigging, and *Sail Training and Cadet Ships,* by Harold A. Underhill (Brown, Son and Ferguson).

Deep Water Sail, by Harold A. Underhill (Sea Breezes Journal of Commerce).

The Last of the Cape Horners, edited by Comdr C. L. A. Woollard RN (A. H. Stockwell).

In addition, and last but by no means least, *all* books by Alan Villiers listed below are veritable storehouses of interest and information to all shiplovers:

Whaling in the Frozen South (Hurst and Blackett).

By Way of Cape Horn (Geoffrey Bles).
Vanished Fleets (Maritime Hist of Tasmania) (Bles).
Sea Dogs of Today (Harrap).
Voyage of the Parma (Bles).
The Sea in Ships, Last of the Windships, The Making of a Sailor (Routledge).
Cruise of the Conrad (Hodders).
Sons of Sinbad (Hodders).
The Coral Sea, The Western Ocean, The Indian Ocean (Museum Press).
The Set of the Sails (Hodders).
Stormalong, Joey Goes to Sea, Pilot Pete (Hodders).

Quest of the Schooner Argus (Hodders).
Posted Missing (Hodders).
The Way of a Ship (Hodders).
Give Me a Ship to Sail (Hodders).
Captain James Cook (Hodders).
The New Mayflower (Brockhampton).
The War with Cape Horn (Hodders).
Of Ships and Men (Newnes).
Pioneers of the Seven Seas (Routledge).
The Battle of Trafalgar (MacMillian, USA).
Bounty Ships of France (with Henri Picard) (Patrick Stephens).
Falmouth for Orders (Patrick Stephens).

Appendix 4

General notes on sailing ship speeds and distances

The highest recorded speed by a sailing ship was 22 knots for four consecutive watches established by the four-masted square-rigged ship *Lancing* whilst on passage to Melbourne in 1890-1. Actually the *Lancing* was built in 1867 as a mail and passenger *steamer* and her original name was *Pereire* and she did in fact serve for 25 years as a steamer before being converted into a full-rigged sailing ship!

Many of the early clipper ships claimed to have exceeded 21 knots, but many of these passages were 'pilot to pilot' records and some doubt must be expressed as to these claims. Both the clipper ships *Thermopylae* and *Cutty Sark* made some astonishingly fast passages and many decades later *Herzogin Cecilie* made what is accepted as the second fastest speed ever recorded by a sailing ship; 20¾ knots. There can, however, be no disputing the claim of *Lancing* as the fastest sailing *ship* ever.

The longest day's run by a sailing ship was 465 nautical miles by the clipper ship *Champion of the Seas* owned by the Liverpool Black Ball Line. This gave an average speed of nearly 20 knots over the whole distance, which is no mean achievement in slightly under 24 hours. The *slowest* sailing ship passage is generally believed to be that of the *Red Rock*, which covered 950 miles in 112 days, which

averages less than 0.4 of a knot!

The fact that *Cutty Sark* is the only complete clipper ship left in the world tends to lead people to believe that she was the fastest, but this is not so. Without a doubt she was one of the best built ships, but she did suffer from bad rudder design and this came unshipped on three occasions. Of course she holds a fond place in every Englishman's heart and she certainly was a most remarkable ship.

There are, according to the best information I can obtain, no fewer than 60 sailing ship wrecks in and around the Falkland Islands and many times that number came to grief off Cape Horn. In fact, so many floundered here that this remote spot was known as the 'Graveyard of the Sailing Ship'. Luckily many sailing ships have been saved and restored including *Balclutha, Viking, Star of India, Wavertree, Polly Woodside, Falls of Clyde* and *Passat*. Many others are still afloat and compete in the Tall Ships Race, such as the *Krusenshtern*, now under the flag of the Soviet Union. This ship was formerly one of the R. F. Laeisz's Flying 'P' line and was built in 1926 as the *Padua*. All Laeisz's ships had names beginning with the letter P. Ships such as *Pommern, Pamir, Parma, Potosi, Priwall, Preussen, Ponape* and *Pinnas* spring readily to mind.

Index